Getting Skills Right

Adult Learning in Italy

WHAT ROLE FOR TRAINING FUNDS ?

OECD
BETTER POLICIES FOR BETTER LIVES

This work is published under the responsibility of the Secretary-General of the OECD. The opinions expressed and arguments employed herein do not necessarily reflect the official views of OECD member countries.

This document, as well as any data and any map included herein, are without prejudice to the status of or sovereignty over any territory, to the delimitation of international frontiers and boundaries and to the name of any territory, city or area.

Please cite this publication as:
OECD (2019), *Adult Learning in Italy: What Role for Training Funds ?*, Getting Skills Right, OECD Publishing, Paris.
https://doi.org/10.1787/9789264311978-en

ISBN 978-92-64-31196-1 (print)
ISBN 978-92-64-31197-8 (pdf)
ISBN 978-92-64-36183-6(HTML)
ISBN 978-92-64-53738-5 (epub)

Getting Skills Right
ISSN 2520-6117 (print)
ISSN 2520-6125 (online)

The statistical data for Israel are supplied by and under the responsibility of the relevant Israeli authorities. The use of such data by the OECD is without prejudice to the status of the Golan Heights, East Jerusalem and Israeli settlements in the West Bank under the terms of international law.

Corrigenda to OECD publications may be found on line at: *www.oecd.org/about/publishing/corrigenda.htm*.

Foreword

The world of work is changing. New technologies, digitalisation, deepening globalisation and population ageing are having a profound impact on the type and quality of jobs that are available and the skills required to do them. To what extent individuals, firms and economies can harness the benefits of these changes critically depends on the readiness of adult learning systems to help people develop relevant skills for this changing world of work.

While Italy has made major progress in the past decade to up-skill its population and workers, further efforts are needed to improve access to good quality adult learning opportunities. Training Funds (i.e. *fondi paritetici interprofessionali per la formazione continua*) represent one important tool through which Italy could face the pressures brought about by the mega-trends, and equip adults and workers with the skills needed to thrive in the labour market and society. This report analyses how Training Funds are designed, used, and monitored, and provides actionable policy recommendations to ensure that they are put to their most effective use.

This report is published under the responsibility of the Secretary-General of the OECD, with the financial assistance of the JPMorgan Chase Foundation. The views expressed in this report should not be taken to reflect the official position of the JPMorgan Chase Foundation.

Acknowledgements

The work on this report was carried out by Alessia Forti from the Skills and Employability Division of the Directorate for Employment, Labour and Social Affairs, under the supervision of Glenda Quintini (Team Manager on Skills) and Mark Keese (Head of the Skills and Employability Division). The report has benefited from helpful comments provided by Andrea Garnero, Fabio Manca, and staff at the JPMorgan Chase Foundation. The Ministry of Labour and Social Affairs (MLPS), the National Agency for Active Labour Market Policies (ANPAL), the National Institute for the Analysis of Public Policies (INAPP), and other stakeholders, provided useful inputs and feedbacks on the report.

Table of contents

Tables

Figures

Boxes

Acronyms and abbreviations

ANPAL	National Agency for Active Labour Market Policies
CGIL, CISL, UIL	The largest trade unions in Italy
CPIA	*Centri Provinciali per l'Istruzione degli Adulti*
CVT	Continuous Vocational Training
EQF	European Qualification Framework
EU	European Union
ICT	Information and communications technology
INAPP	National Institute for the Analysis of Public Policies
INPS	National Institute for Social Security
MLPS	The Ministry of Labour and Social Affairs
NQF	National Qualification Framework
OHS	Occupational Health and Safety
PES	Public Employment Service
PIAAC	Programme for the International Assessment of Adult Competencies
SAA	Skills Assessment and Anticipation
SME	Small and medium-sized enterprises
TF	Training fund
UN	United Nations

Executive summary

Action on the adult learning front is needed urgently in Italy. As a result of the introduction of new technologies, 15.2% of jobs have a high risk of automation, and a further 35.5% may experience significant changes to how they are performed. Italy also has an old and ageing population. Today there are 3.5 older persons (65+) for every ten working age adults (15-64) – the highest rate in the OECD after Japan. Finally, around 38% of Italian adults have low levels of literacy and/or numeracy proficiency, well above the OECD average of 26.3%.

To cope with technological change, longer working lives and the increased skill demands of a knowledge-based economy, many adults will need training to keep skills up to date. However, the Italian adult learning system seems to be ill prepared to face these challenges. Today, only two in ten adults participate in job-related training, about half the OECD average. Moreover, only 60.2% of firms (with at least 10 employees) provide training to their workers, lower than the OECD European average of 76%.

Training Funds represent one important tool through which Italy could face the pressures brought about by the mega-trends, and equip adults and workers with the skills needed to thrive in the labour market and society. Instituted in the early 2000s, today Training Funds cover almost 1 million firms and over 10 million workers, and manage more than EUR 600 million a year, representing one of the most important sources of financing for workers' continuous learning in Italy.

Since their inception, Training Funds have encouraged many firms to train their workers, and have certainly contributed to improve access to training opportunities. However, there are challenges. SMEs still face substantial barriers in adhering to/using Training Funds, and many vulnerable groups – such as the low-skilled, low-wage workers or older people – are often excluded from the training opportunities offered.

Moreover, training is not always of good quality and aligned to the needs of the labour market. Indeed, Training Funds are often used to finance compulsory training, such as occupational health and safety, rather than focussing on developing the skills that could enhance the competitiveness of firms and the productivity of workers.

What is more, in recent years, Training Funds have been the object of significant budget curtailments by the government, raising concerns on the financial adequacy and sustainability of the system.

Finally, another key challenge is that often Training Funds work in silos, with scattered coordination efforts taking place among Training Funds themselves and with other actors involved in adult learning.

To ensure that Training Funds are put to their most effective use, the OECD recommends to:

- **Increase training participation among SMEs and vulnerable workers,** for example by fostering a learning culture among SMEs; further reducing red tape and training costs for SMEs; training entrepreneurs; and putting in place targeted initiatives to ensure that training reaches disadvantaged groups.

- **Align training to the skills needed in the labour market,** for example by strengthening the involvement of social partners in training decisions; making better use of skills assessment and anticipation exercises; helping firms and workers to understand their training needs; and forbidding the use of Training Funds for compulsory training.
- **Ensure that training is of good quality**, for example by streamlining quality-monitoring procedures; strengthening skills certification; fostering a healthy competitive environment among Training Funds; strengthening the information system; and evaluating the impact of training more systematically.
- **Enhance coordination among different actors**, for example by setting up a National Observatory on Adult Learning; formalising the coordination between Training Funds; and setting up complementary policies to develop a learning-friendly environment.
- **Ensure that Training Funds receive adequate and sustainable funding**, by minimising governments' withdrawals for purposes other than training. Moreover, the levy rate could be increased (at the national level or through collective agreements) and the additional rate could be made refundable with a view to contain firms' labour costs.

Assessment and Recommendations

Mega-trends are putting pressures on the Italian adult learning system

Technological change, population ageing and low levels of basic skills among adults, are putting serious pressure on the Italian adult learning system. In Italy, 15.2% of jobs have a high risk of automation, and a further 35.5% may experience significant changes to how they are performed as a result of the introduction of new technologies. Italy also has an old and ageing population. Today there are 3.5 older persons (65+) for every ten working age adults (15-64) – the highest rate in the OECD after Japan – and this ratio is expected to increase to 6.6 by 2050. Finally, around 38% of Italian adults have low levels of literacy and/or numeracy proficiency, well above the OECD average of 26.3%. To cope with technological change, longer working lives and the increased skill demands of a knowledge-based economy, many adults will need training to keep skills up to date. In this context, the availability of high-quality adult learning options is crucial to support workers through these ongoing and deep changes.

Participation into adult learning has increased over the last decade but remains low

Adults' participation in training has increased considerably in Italy over the past decade, rising by 133% over the period 2007-2016. Despite this progress, Italy continues to lag behind most OECD countries, and too many adults – including the most vulnerable – do not participate in adult learning opportunities. Today, only two in ten adults participate in job-related training (about half the OECD average) and, although the low-skilled are arguably those who are in most need of training, only 9.5% participate (OECD average is around 20%).

Training Funds can play an important role in upskilling the Italian workforce

The Italian Training Funds (i.e. *fondi paritetici interprofessionali per la formazione continua*, hereafter TFs) are associations run by social partners that finance workers' training, using resources collected through a training levy imposed on employers. Since their introduction in 2004, they have been tasked to encourage firms to provide training to their workers, and have likely contributed to the significant increase in adult learning participation recorded since then. Covering almost 1 million firms and over 10 million workers, and managing over EUR 600 million a year, today Training Funds represent one of the most important sources of financing for workers' continuous learning in Italy. If well used, Training Funds can help Italy address the challenges brought about by the mega-trends, and equip adults and workers with the skills needed to thrive in the labour market.

Changes in the legal framework have modified the way Training Funds operate and function

Since the establishment of Training Funds, there have been various debates regarding whether the funding they manage is public or private. The norms that originally regulated the activities of the Training Funds were opaque around this point, and this legal vacuum has led to the proliferation of different interpretations of the rules. To put an end to this long-lasting uncertainty, in 2016 the Ministry of Labour and Social Affairs bound the Training Funds to the Law on State Aids and Public Procurement Legislation – effectively making Training Funds public entities. On the one hand, the new rules have improved accountability, and pushed Training Funds to rethink their strategies. On the other hand, however, they have put additional administrative burdens on Training Funds – possibly slowing down their activities, crowding out resources to finance training, and making Training Funds a much less flexible instrument overall.

Training Funds may need more resources to cope with rising pressure on the skills system

The training levy paid by Italian employers is low by international standards. In Italy, the levy amounts to 0.3% of payroll compared with 0.8% in Ireland, up to 1% in France, 1.5% in Hungary, up to 2% in the Netherlands, and up to 2.5% in the United Kingdom. This relatively low funding level puts into question the ability of Training Funds to cope with rising skill pressures. Further, in recent years the Italian government has diverted part of TF resources to uses other than training: in 2017, out of the EUR 735 million collected, only 58.9% were transferred to Training Funds, in practice reducing the funding available to Training Funds to only 0.19-0.2% of the payroll. While funds were initially diverted to finance welfare measures in response to the challenges brought about by the economic crisis, from 2015 onwards government withdrawals have become structural. In a context of high skill pressures, a reduction in resources available to invest in continuous learning is something that Italy can ill-afford. Besides reducing resources for training, budget cuts may also affect Training Funds' credibility, undermine overall trust in the system, and ultimately discourage firms to join or remain enrolled in a Training Fund.

Ensuring that Training Funds receive adequate and sustainable funding. Governments' withdrawal for purposes other than training should be minimised in the future. The levy rate could be increased at the national level, by law, or through collective agreements. The additional rate could be made refundable to contain labour costs.

SMEs face several barriers to providing training and using funding support available

While a large and growing number of firms are covered by Training Funds, certain firms (e.g. SMEs) still face substantial barriers in adhering to/using the schemes. Like in other OECD countries, SMEs in Italy are less likely to train their workers compared to larger firms. In 2016, only 57.1% of small firms (10-19 employees) provided training, compared to 93.3% of larger firms (250+ employees). Moreover, even those SMEs that supply training use available Training Funds funding much less than larger companies. Interestingly, only 6.2% of small training firms (10-19 employees) receive financial support from training funds, compared to 64.1% of larger firms (1000+ employees). High direct and indirect cost of training, lack of a learning culture among entrepreneurs of small businesses, poor awareness of the availability of Training Funds funding, as well as burdensome administrative procedures to apply for funding, are among the factors explaining the limited use of Training Funds funding by smaller firms.

- *Reducing the direct cost of training for SMEs.* Several policy options are available, such as: (i) granting SMEs higher reimbursement rates; (ii) shortening/removing delays in reimbursements; (iii) exempting, or reducing, contributions paid by SMEs.
- *Decreasing the opportunity costs of training for SMEs,* for example by (i) reimbursing firms for workers' wages during training; (ii) introducing job rotation schemes (*i.e.* support firms to find a temporary replacement worker during the training period).
- *Fostering a learning culture among SMEs*, for example by upskilling entrepreneurs through Training Funds. Training could be financed through entrepreneurs' private contributions, and/or government funding.
- *Raising awareness among SMEs about Training Funds.* The government could lead information awareness campaigns; social partners could disseminate information about Training Funds among their networks; Training Funds could build on existing networks (*e.g.* trade associations) to reach both member and non-member firms.
- *Easing administrative procedures and red tape.* SMEs could benefit from a simplified funding application procedure, which would require them to describe training needs and expected outcomes, rather than to develop detailed training plans.

Vulnerable groups are sometimes excluded from training opportunities

In Italy, as in other countries, the most vulnerable adults – such as the low-skilled, low-wage workers or older people – are less likely to participate to training. There is an open debate on whether (and to what extent) the low participation of vulnerable groups should be addressed by Training Funds or via other instruments of public nature (e.g. European Social Fund; regional funds). Indeed, as training is funded through a levy paid by employers, there is resistance in excessively limiting or steering firms' decisions on how to use the funds. As a result, firms typically have a great deal of autonomy in deciding who gets training, and often end up targeting training efforts to groups for which training yields the highest returns: the most skilled, those in high-skilled occupations, or younger workers with longer career prospects.

Whether Training Funds should explicitly target vulnerable groups who otherwise would receive little training remains an issue of open debate, which requires a reflection on the role that Training Funds should play in the labour market and society. For the time being, while some Training Funds have been taking steps to ensure that training reaches the most vulnerable workers, efforts have been far from systematic. Only few grants are exclusively dedicated to vulnerable workers or give them priority access. Similarly, individual training plans – Training Funds financing channels conceived to address the specific needs of individual workers – are the least frequently used type of training (representing only 1.6%

of participants) and rarely serve the purpose of reaching the vulnerable. Moreover, for disadvantaged workers to use them, individual training plans need to be accompanied with skills assessments procedures, guidance services, and skills certification, which are not always provided. E-learning training represents another tool through which Training Funds could reach workers with specific barriers to learning, but its use is limited as it currently reaches only 11.8% of all participants.

- *Ensuring that training reaches the most vulnerable.* This could be done in several ways: (i) devoting part of the funding to vulnerable workers (e.g. by giving them priority or developing dedicated grants); (ii) using *individual training plans* more broadly; (iii) investing in support measures (e.g. skills assessment; guidance; certification) to facilitate training take-up by the most vulnerable.
- *Expanding e-learning opportunities.* In order to ensure take-up of e-learning, adults need to be equipped with good basic skills (e.g. ICT); and Training Funds need to be adequately equipped to monitor and evaluate the successful delivery of e-learning programmes (*e.g.* through – *ex-ante*, *in itinere* and *ex-post* examinations to test the competences acquired; and/or through skills certification).

Training is not always aligned to the skills most demanded in the labour market

In order for Training Funds to fulfil their mandate, not only do they need to ensure a broad coverage of firms and workers, but they also need to provide training that is useful and aligned to labour market needs. While Training Funds have the potential to equip workers with the skills needed to adapt to the challenges arising from the mega-trends, a relatively large share of the training they provide does not support the development of in-demand skills. For example, compulsory Occupational Health and Safety (OHS) training represents over 30% of all TF-supported training activities, while ICT training accounts for just above 3%. Indeed, while it is forbidden to use *collective accounts* to finance OHS, it is still possible for firms to finance OHS training through their *individual accounts*. Using Training Funds to finance compulsory OHS training risks generating large deadweight losses (*i.e.* financing training that would have taken place even in the absence of the subsidy), on top of representing a missed opportunity to provide workers with the skills needed to adapt to future labour market challenges.

There are several explanations behind this suboptimal use of resources. Some firms are unable to understand their training needs and develop plans accordingly, and as a result they may turn to OHS training which is easier to plan. Firms also dispose of limited time to spend funding before resources feed back to the Training Funds, which may push them to exhaust unspent resources on OHS training. Moreover, Training Funds financing is often seen by firms as a mean to relieve the costs associated with compulsory training obligations, which, especially in a context of high labour costs, would be otherwise hard to cover solely through private resources. Finally, the high focus on OHS training also reflects the productive structure of the Italian economy, characterised by many small family-led businesses, which are often more concerned about complying with compulsory training obligations than developing skills (e.g. ICT) which may take time to pay off.

- *Equipping workers with ICT skills needed for the digital transformation.* All Training Funds could develop a dedicated budget line for technological innovation; and/or give a higher score to training plans that include a technological innovation component (e.g. skills required under Industry 4.0).
- *Forbidding the use of Training Funds funding for compulsory training, such as occupational health and safety (OHS).* This prohibition needs to be coupled with complementary policies to (i) monitor that firms continue to provide compulsory training; (ii) help firms perceive OHS as a civic obligation; (iii) lengthen the time available for firms to use funding in *individual accounts* so that they can develop thorough training plans.

Social dialogue around training could be improved

One way to ensure that training aligns to skills needs is to ensure that social partners' views are reflected in the various phases of TF-supported training provision. In theory, legislation gives social partners the means to influence the TF training agenda at all stages: the management board of TFs must be composed by representatives of social partners; all training proposals must be agreed between social partner representatives; and no plan can be submitted for funding without approval from trade unions' representatives. Moreover, some Training Funds have even set up a dedicated committee, where social partners meet on a regular basis to jointly identify the key skills priorities of the Training Fund and determine how to best use resources available.

In practice, however, social dialogue can be improved further. The fragmentation of the Italian social partners system (Italy has the 2nd highest number of employers' organisations and trade unions in the OECD) means that coming to an agreement on training priorities can be challenging. Further, extensive use of *individual accounts* – accounts that firms can directly use to finance their own training, with little intermediation of Training Funds – risks weakening social dialogue and reducing Training Funds to a mere "cash dispenser". Good stand-alone initiatives aside, involvement by trade unions has also proved difficult. Training plans are often developed by firms, employers' organisations, or training providers, while the involvement of trade unions is at cases only formal. Sometimes ill-prepared to understand workers' skills needs, struggling to make their voice heard by firms, and pressured to prioritise other non-learning related issues (e.g. job redundancy; job contracts) in the context of the economic crisis, trade unions have sometimes found it challenging to effectively influence training content.

Strengthening the involvement of social partners in training decisions. There are several policy options, including: (i) training trade unionists to better understand workers' skills needs; (ii) prioritising skills issues in the collective bargaining agenda; (iii) establishing new positions for trade union training specialists.

Training often reflects what providers are able to offer, rather than what firms and workers need

TF-supported training is still often supply-oriented, i.e. it reflects what training providers are able to offer, rather than what firms and workers actually need. This is partly due to the fact that Training Funds, firms and workers are themselves not well-aware of labour market training needs. In order to ensure that training is demand-driven and responds to the real needs of firms and workers, it is important that Training Funds make the best use of existing Skills Assessment and Anticipation (SAA) information, and help firms and workers identifying their needs. Despite many good efforts, more action is needed in this direction. In fact, although Italy produces a wealth of SAA information, results are sometimes not fit for purpose or not easily accessible by Training Funds. And while many Training Funds are guiding firms and workers in their training efforts, more needs to be done, as the vast majority (93.7%) of all TF-supported training programmes are still not integrated by any career guidance or skills assessment activity.

- *Making better use of existing skills assessment and anticipation (SAA) exercises to establish training priorities*. Existing SAA information – already very rich and comprehensive in Italy – should be used systematically by all Training Funds to establish training priorities and orient their strategies.
- *Assisting firms and workers to understand their skills and training needs*. ANPAL could, for example: (i) make it compulsory for all training plans to be based on the analysis of skills needs; (ii) encourage Training Funds to give a premium to training plans, based on the quality of the skills analysis; (iii) develop an app/online tool to help firms and workers assess their current and future skills needs. This app/online tool could also help ANPAL collect systematic information on skills needs across TF-member firms and workers.

Training Funds dispose of a wide range of tools to ensure training quality, but no strict quality standards exist

Ensuring that training is of good quality is essential to ensure it achieves its objectives and is useful. While Training Funds dispose of a wide range of tools to ensure quality, no strict training quality standards exist. For example, each Training Fund has its own accreditation strategy to ensure that funding goes to training providers that are of good quality, with some Training Funds relying on regional accreditation systems, and others developing their own accreditation criteria. Similarly, funding allocation procedures vary greatly across Training Funds, with some outsourcing assessment procedures to external committees, and others evaluating training plans internally. While this variety of practices gives Training Funds a great deal of autonomy and flexibility, it also risks generating large differences in the quality of training provided, create uncertainty around how quality should be defined and assessed, and ultimately undermine the transparency of the system.

Streamlining quality-monitoring procedures. For example, (i) regional accreditation systems could be harmonised, based on a set of similar quality standards; (ii) funding allocation procedures could be streamlined, *e.g.* by making it compulsory for all Training Funds to rely on an external, independent, committee to assess training plans.

An increasing share of training is being certified, but the system remains fragmented

Italy has devoted significant efforts to improve its skills certification system. The government developed a National Qualification Framework, which creates a national "taxonomy" to link regional qualification frameworks with one another; ANPAL, with its recently published guidelines, has set forth the rules to make skills certification of TF-supported training easy and possible at all times; Training Funds and social partners have promoted successful initiatives to encourage skills certification. Reflecting these good efforts, the share of participants to TF-supported training who receive a certification rose from 48.8% in 2014 to 61.8% in 2016. Despite the progress made, however, a large share of TF-supported training still remains uncertified, and the vast array of actors involved in skills certification practices means that the system is quite fragmented. One key challenge is the incompatibility between regional certification systems and TF-supported training. For example, some regional certification systems mainly relate to "low-skilled professions", that are ill-suited for TF-supported training that also reaches workers in "high-skilled occupations". As another example, regional certification is often issued upon completion of a formal, long-term, training programme – while much of TF-supported training is non-formal and of shorter duration. On top of this incompatibility, another key challenge in Italy is the perception that skills certification is a low-status practice reserved for the low-skilled, which may discourage workers to undertake certification procedures.

Strengthening skills certification further. Continue implementing ANPAL Guidelines but also (i) set a minimum training duration, so as to ensure that the (short) length of training courses does not compromise certification; (ii) ensure that each training plan is designed to explicitly refer to a specific skills certification system (e.g. regional; TF certification).

Competition among Training Funds does not always translate into better quality services

Training Funds are in competition with one another, partly because firms are allowed to enrol in the Training Fund of their choosing and/or switch to a different Training Fund virtually at any time (regardless of their economic sector). While in theory a certain amount of competition is desirable as it may push Training Funds to improve the quality of their services, in practice this does not happen. Training Funds often try to attract firms by easing administrative procedures, or by giving firms more independence on how to use funding, rather than focussing on training quality. Further, until recently, Training Funds have operated in an uncertain legal framework, which has also contributed to shaping an unhealthy competitive environment. Steps in the right direction are already being implemented to address these challenges – for example ANPAL has recently developed guidelines to make all Training Funds play by a clear, and shared, set of rules.

Fostering a healthy competitive environment among Training Funds. Different policy options are available, such as: (i) reducing the number of Training Funds, for example by merging some of the smaller or less performing Training Funds; (ii) linking each Training Fund to an economic sector; (iii) setting minimum operational standards.

There is room to make the monitoring and evaluation system more thorough

Collecting information on the activities of Training Funds is fundamental to monitor who is benefiting from training, understand whether resources are being well invested, and keep track of progress. While an information system is in place to regularly collect data on the activities of the Training Funds, it has several limitations. For example, no information is collected at the individual and firm level, which generates double counting and limits data analysis. Moreover, information feeds into the information system in scattered ways, which can bias the results and ultimately undermine data elaboration. Some aspects of the activities of the Training Funds are currently overlooked (e.g. training quality), or not explored extensively enough (e.g. skills certification), which highlights the potential to make the information system more thorough. Finally, the information system is not linked to other adult learning databases (e.g. regional), making it difficult for policy makers to monitor whether adult learning efforts duplicate or complement each other. Another key challenge relates to the (lack of an) impact evaluation culture. While some Training Funds have taken laudable steps to measure the impact that training has on firms and workers, what is still missing in Italy is a systematic effort to measure the benefits of training.

- *Strengthening the information system.* The existing information system could be improved with a view to (i) collect data at the individual (participant/firm) level; (ii) collect more information and at a higher level of disaggregation; (iii) better link to other adult learning databases.
- *Evaluating the impact of training.* Evaluation efforts should be systematic, regular, and objective; they could be carried out by institutional bodies (ANPAL; INAPP); outsourced to independent evaluators; and/or conducted by Training Funds themselves. Evaluations could draw from subjective data (e.g. firms/participants' satisfaction) or more objective measures.

Training Funds often work in silos and coordination efforts could be strengthened

Ensuring that each Training Fund coordinates with different actors involved in adult learning can bring several advantages. It could give Training Funds opportunities for dialogue, cooperation, and sharing of good practices; limit overlap/duplication of interventions and ensure that training reaches the most vulnerable; and help Training Funds participate in the policy dialogue and ensure that their concerns and priorities are reflected in the policy agenda. Yet, too often, Training Funds work in silos. Interactions across Training Funds remain most often ad-hoc, informal, and largely dependent on the goodwill of management board members, with limited institutional/formal opportunities to meet on a systematic basis. There are also few institutional linkages between Training Funds and *Centri Provinciali per l'Istruzione degli Adulti* or Public Employment Services, while dialogue between Training Funds and regions is mainly limited to the sharing of information and, in sporadic cases, co-programming of grants. Coordination with government institutions is also rather unsystematic. A National Observatory on Adult Learning was originally conceived in 2004 with the aim of improving coordination among different actors, but it was soon after abandoned and is currently not operational.

- *Setting up a National Observatory on Adult Learning* to facilitate coordination between Training Funds, the government, and other actors involved in adult learning. The Observatory could organise regular meetings to discuss important topics (results of SAA; skills certification) and/or steer the development of a national adult learning strategy.
- *Improving coordination between Training Funds.* Training Funds could establish a coordination platform to share good practices, discuss common challenges, and collaborate on new projects.

Training Funds could play a central role in training the unemployed but they need to be supported

During the economic crisis, Training Funds played an important role in helping the unemployed/displaced workers to retrain and reintegrate the labour market. This meant expanding beyond their traditional beneficiaries (the employed) towards the unemployed – under a legal framework that was not conceived for this purpose. While Training Funds efforts during the crisis have been remarkable, today the bulk of Training Funds activities remains focussed on the employed population. Indeed, training for permanent and temporary workers absorbs over 87% of all TF-supported training programmes. Going forward, if Training Funds are called to play a more concerted role in the re-skilling of the unemployed, the legal framework will need updating and additional financial resources will need to be allocated to ensure that Training Funds can successfully take on the new responsibilities. The Jobs Act already takes step in this direction, but it remains to be seen how these measures will be implemented in practice.

Paving the way for Training Funds to support the training of the unemployed. Updating the legal framework and allocating adequate additional resources will be crucial for Training Funds to successfully undertake this new role.

Strengthening complementary policies for a more learning-friendly environment

There is only so much that Training Funds can do to ensure that adult learning opportunities are inclusive, of good quality, and well aligned to skills needs. On top of improving how Training Funds operate and function, complementary policies need to be implemented by the government. In the future, it will be important that the government implements policies to remove workers' barriers to training (more generous paid education and training leave; financial incentives for workers to take-up training; link wages more closely to productivity), as well as industrial policies to raise firms' demand for high-level skills. While these policies typically fall outside the responsibility of Training Funds, they are fundamental to ensure that Training Funds can work effectively.

Setting up complementary policies to develop a learning-friendly environment. Policy measures aimed at removing workers' barriers to training (e.g. education/training leave; financial incentives for workers to take-up training; Individual Learning Accounts; individual rights to learning), and demand-side measures to increase firms' demand for skills, should be explored.

Summary of key recommendations

Increasing training participation among SMEs and vulnerable workers

- *Reducing the direct cost of training for SMEs.* Several policy options are available, such as: (i) granting SMEs higher reimbursement rates; (ii) shortening/removing delays in reimbursements; (iii) exempting, or reducing, contributions paid by SMEs.
- *Decreasing the opportunity costs of training for SMEs,* for example by (i) reimbursing firms for workers' wages during training; (ii) introducing job rotation schemes (*i.e.* support firms to find a temporary replacement worker during the training period).
- *Fostering a learning culture among SMEs*, for example by upskilling entrepreneurs through Training Funds. Training could be financed through entrepreneurs' private contributions, and/or government funding.
- *Raising awareness among SMEs about Training Funds.* The government could lead information awareness campaigns; social partners could disseminate information about Training Funds among their networks; Training Funds could build on existing networks (*e.g.* trade associations) to reach both member and non-member firms.
- *Easing administrative procedures and red tape.* SMEs could benefit from a simplified funding application procedure, which would require them to describe training needs and expected outcomes, rather than to develop detailed training plans.
- *Ensuring that training reaches the most vulnerable.* This could be done in several ways: (i) devoting part of the funding to vulnerable workers (e.g. by giving them priority or developing dedicated grants); (ii) using *individual training plans* more broadly; (iii) investing in support measures (e.g. skills assessment; guidance; certification) to facilitate training take-up by the most vulnerable.
- *Expanding e-learning opportunities*. In order to ensure take-up of e-learning, adults need to be equipped with good basic skills (e.g. ICT); and Training Funds need to be adequately equipped to monitor and evaluate the successful delivery of e-learning programmes (*e.g.* through – *ex-ante*, *in itinere* and *ex-post* examinations to test the competences acquired; and/or through skills certification).

Aligning training to the skills needed in the labour market

- *Strengthening the involvement of social partners in training decisions.* There are several policy options, including: (i) training trade unionists to better understand workers' skills needs; (ii) prioritising skills issues in the collective bargaining agenda; (iii) establishing new positions for trade union training specialists.
- *Making better use of existing skills assessment and anticipation (SAA) exercises to establish training priorities*. Existing SAA information – already very rich and comprehensive in Italy – should be used systematically by all Training Funds to establish training priorities and orient their strategies.

- *Assisting firms and workers to understand their skills and training needs*. ANPAL could, for example: (i) make it compulsory for all training plans to be based on the analysis of skills needs; (ii) encourage Training Funds to give a premium to training plans, based on the quality of the skills analysis; (iii) develop an app/online tool to help firms and workers assess their current and future skills needs. This app/online tool could also help ANPAL collect systematic information on skills needs across TF-member firms and workers.
- *Equipping workers with ICT skills needed for the digital transformation.* All Training Funds could develop a dedicated budget line for technological innovation; and/or give a higher score to training plans that include a technological innovation component (e.g. skills required under Industry 4.0).
- *Forbidding the use of Training Funds funding for compulsory training, such as occupational health and safety (OHS)*. This prohibition needs to be coupled with complementary policies to (i) monitor that firms continue to provide compulsory training; (ii) help firms perceive OHS as a civic obligation; (iii) lengthen the time available for firms to use funding in *individual accounts* so that they can develop thorough training plans.

Ensuring that training is of good quality

- *Streamlining quality-monitoring procedures.* For example, (i) regional accreditation systems could be harmonised, based on a set of similar quality standards; (ii) funding allocation procedures could be streamlined, *e.g.* by making it compulsory for all Training Funds to rely on an external, independent, committee to assess training plans.
- *Strengthening skills certification further.* Continue implementing ANPAL Guidelines but also (i) set a minimum training duration, so as to ensure that the (short) length of training courses does not compromise certification; (ii) ensure that each training plan is designed to explicitly refer to a specific skills certification system (e.g. regional; TF certification).
- *Fostering a healthy competitive environment among Training Funds.* Different policy options are available, such as: (i) reducing the number of Training Funds, for example by merging some of the smaller or less performing Training Funds; (ii) linking each Training Fund to an economic sector; (iii) setting minimum operational standards.
- *Strengthening the information system.* The existing information system could be improved with a view to (i) collect data at the individual (participant/firm) level; (ii) collect more information and at a higher level of disaggregation; (iii) better link to other adult learning databases.
- *Evaluating the impact of training*. Evaluation efforts should be systematic, regular, and objective; they could be carried out by institutional bodies (ANPAL; INAPP); outsourced to independent evaluators; and/or conducted by Training Funds themselves. Evaluations could draw from subjective data (e.g. firms/participants' satisfaction) or more objective measures.

Enhancing coordination among different actors

- *Setting up a National Observatory on Adult Learning* to facilitate coordination between Training Funds, the government, and other actors involved in adult learning. The Observatory could organise regular meetings to discuss important topics (results of SAA; skills certification) and/or steer the development of a national adult learning strategy.
- *Improving coordination between Training Funds.* Training Funds could establish a coordination platform to share good practices, discuss common challenges, and collaborate on new projects.
- *Paving the way for Training Funds to support the training of the unemployed.* Updating the legal framework and allocating adequate additional resources will be crucial for Training Funds to successfully undertake this new role.
- *Setting up complementary policies to develop a learning-friendly environment.* Policy measures aimed at removing workers' barriers to training (e.g. education/training leave; financial incentives for workers to take-up training; Individual Learning Accounts; individual rights to learning), and demand-side measures to increase firms' demand for skills, should be explored.
- *Ensuring that Training Funds receive adequate and sustainable funding.* Governments' withdrawal for purposes other than training should be minimised in the future. The levy rate could be increased at the national level, by law, or through collective agreements. The additional rate could be made refundable to contain labour costs.

Chapter 1. The context: Why is adult learning important in Italy?

In Italy, as in other OECD countries, demographic change, globalisation, and technological progress are having a profound impact on skills needs. Italy has an old and rapidly ageing population, and over half of workers may see their job tasks change significantly as a result of automation. In addition, a large share of adults has relatively low skills. Within this context, the availability of adult learning options of high quality is crucial to support workers through these ongoing, deep, and rapid changes. However, while the share of adults participating in job-related learning in Italy has increased substantially over the past years compared to other OECD countries, participation remains low, especially for those who need training the most. This chapter analyses the key drivers of skills pressures, placing Italy into the international context.

The statistical data for Israel are supplied by and under the responsibility of the relevant Israeli authorities. The use of such data by the OECD is without prejudice to the status of the Golan Heights, East Jerusalem and Israeli settlements in the West Bank under the terms of international law.

1.1. Adults' skills

In Italy, a large share of adults has low skills. Around 38% of Italian adults have low levels of literacy and/or numeracy proficiency, a share larger than in all but two other OECD countries (Chile and Turkey) with available data, and well above the average of 26.3% (see Figure 1.1). The situation does not improve much at workplaces. Indeed, 33.6% of workers in Italy have low literacy and/or numeracy proficiency, a share that is higher than most OECD countries with the only exception of Chile, Greece and Turkey, and well above the OECD average of 22.7% (see Figure 1.1). These adults may struggle to find a place in the labour market, and when at work they may find it hard to access productive job opportunities.

Figure 1.1. The proportion of low performers in literacy and/or numeracy

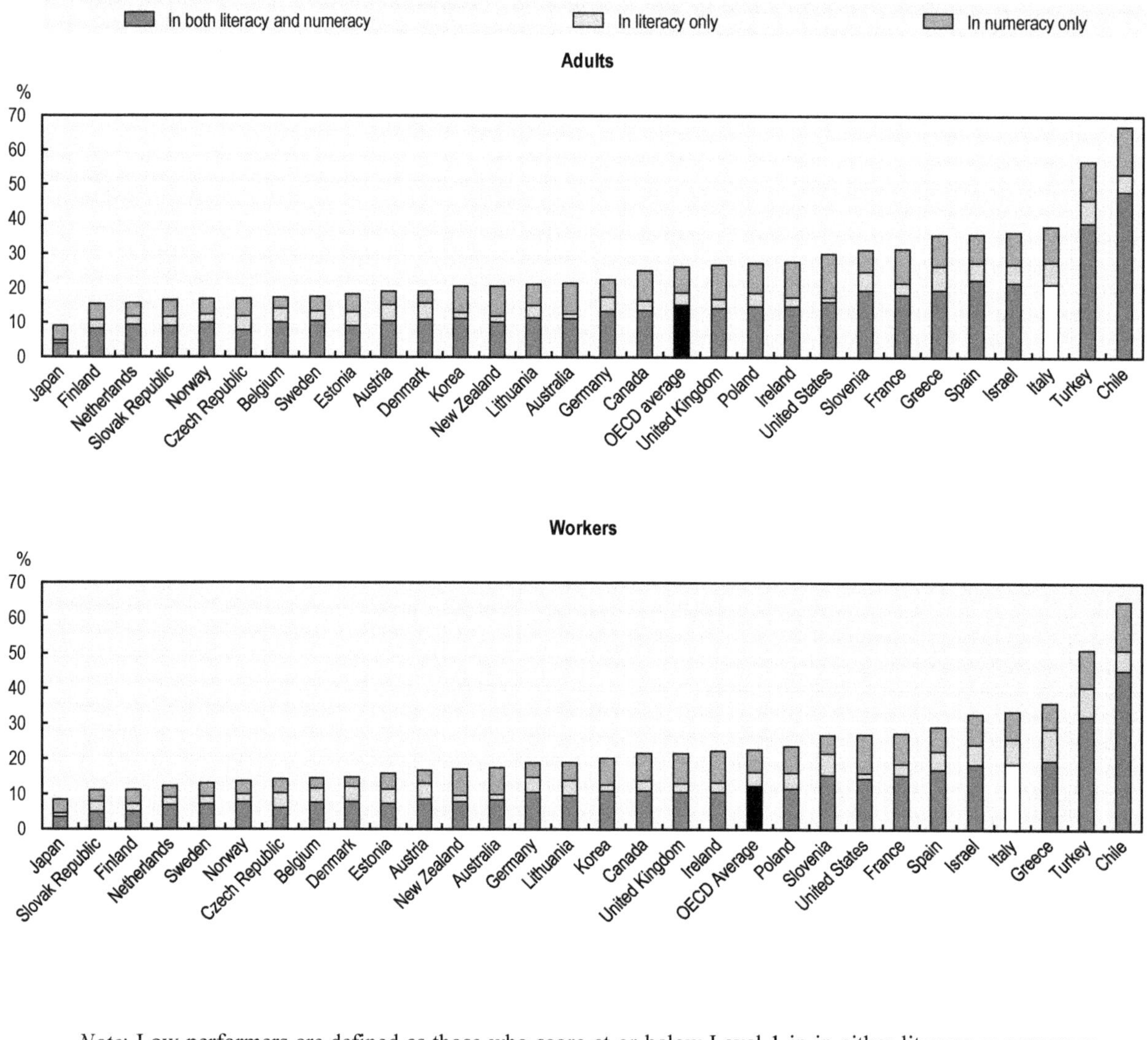

Note: Low-performers are defined as those who score at or below Level 1 in in either literacy or numeracy according to the Survey of Adult Skills. Chile, Greece, Israel, New Zealand, Slovenia and Turkey: Year of reference 2015. All other countries: Year of reference 2012. Data for Belgium refer only to Flanders and data for the United Kingdom refer to England and Northern Ireland jointly.
Source: OECD calculations based on the Survey of Adult Skills (PIAAC) (2012 and 2015).

1.2. Risk of automation

New technologies are changing jobs and skill needs, in Italy like elsewhere in the OECD. While on the one hand these new technologies have the potential to free up workers' time to do more productive and less routine jobs, on the other hand they will likely change many existing jobs and the skills required to perform them. Indeed, recent OECD research (Nedelkoska and Quintini, 2018[1]) suggests that in Italy 15.2% of jobs have a high risk of automation, and a further 35.5% of jobs may experience significant changes to how they are performed. This risk is higher than the average of OECD countries with available data (14% and 31.6% for the two indicators, respectively) (see Figure 1.2). This puts considerable pressures on the Italian adult learning system, as many individuals will need to re-skill to cope with the change.

Figure 1.2. Jobs at risk of automation or significant change

Percentage of jobs at risk by degree of risk

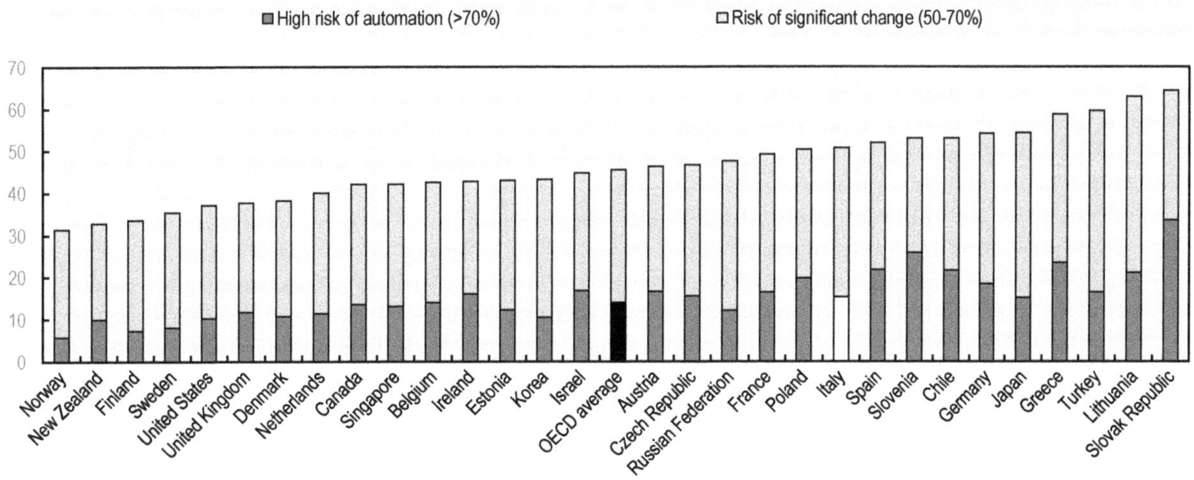

Source: Nedelkoska and Quintini (2018[1]).

1.3. Population ageing

Italy also has an old and ageing population, which puts further pressures on its adult learning system. According to UN population statistics, Italy has only 2.6 times as many working-age adults than over-65-year-olds today – making Italy the second most "aged" country in the OECD, after Japan – and this number will shrink to 1.5 by 2050 (see Figure 1.3). These demographic trends can impact training needs in a number of important ways. They may increase the need for individuals to update their skills over the life-course in a context of longer working lives. The retirement of large cohorts can lead to significant shortages of labour, a gap that can be filled through up- and re-skilling of the existing workforce. Finally, population ageing can result in further shifts in the demand for goods and services, e.g. increased demand for health and care services, which may require substantial up-skilling of the existing workforce (OECD, 2019[2]).

Figure 1.3. Population ageing

Population aged 65+ as % of population aged 15-64

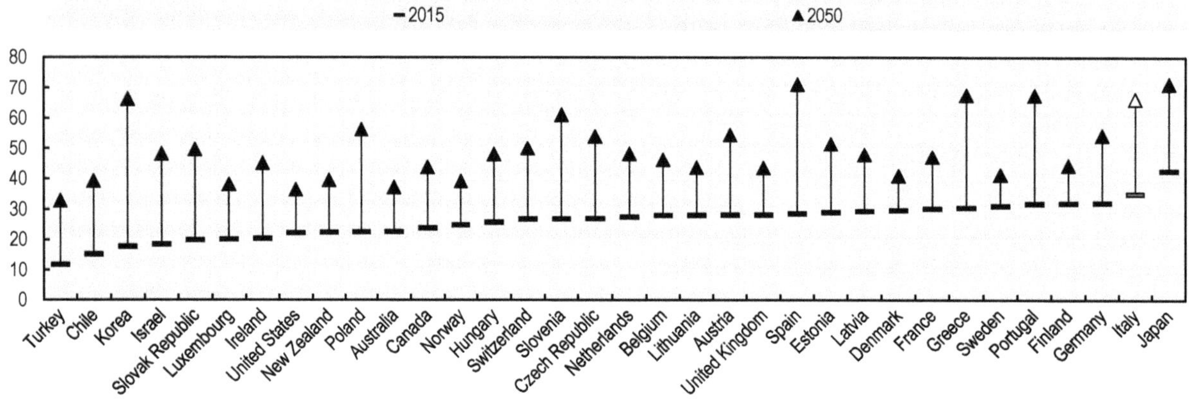

Source: UN population statistics.

1.4. Participation to adult learning

In this context, the availability of adult learning options of high quality is crucial to support workers through these ongoing, deep, and rapid changes. Adults' participation to and firms' provision of training opportunities has improved considerably in Italy over the past decade, although from a low initial base. Indeed, elaborations of the Adult Education Survey show that the share of adults participating in job-related learning in Italy has increased by 133% between 2007 and 2016, the second highest increase in OECD European countries after Hungary. Similarly, elaborations of the Continuing Vocational Training Survey show that the share of firms providing training to their workers has increased by 87% in Italy between 2005 and 2015, the second highest increase after Latvia (see Figure 1.4).

Figure 1.4. Trends in adults' participation and firms' provision of training, Italy and OECD countries

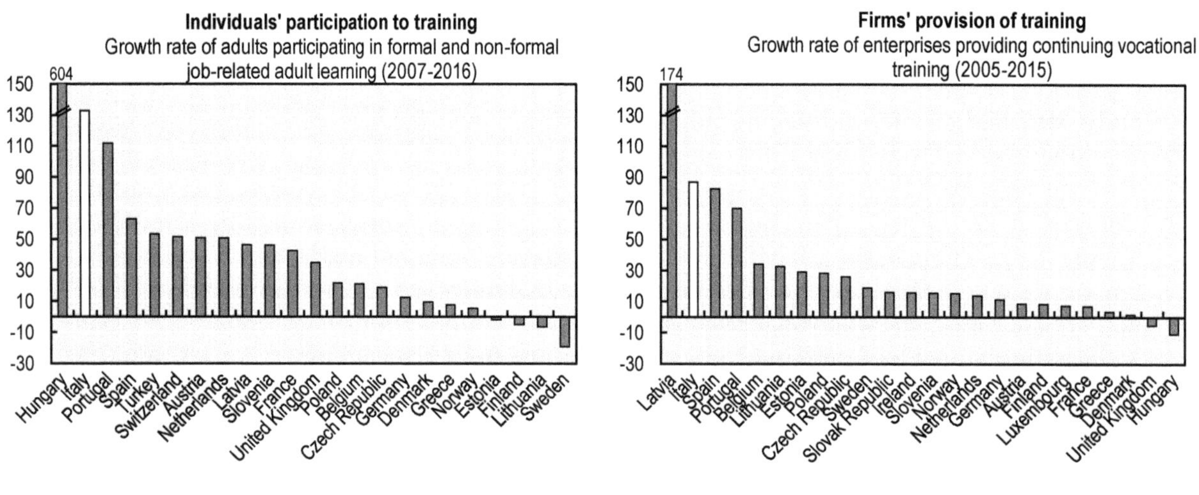

Source: AES and CVTS; data for Australia refer to WRTAL; data for New Zealand refers to the Business Operations Survey.

Despite this progress, however, Italy continues to lag behind by international standards. Too many adults – including the low-skilled – still do not participate in adult learning opportunities and a high share of firms continue not to provide any training to their workers. Indeed, PIAAC data shows how in Italy only 20.1% of the adult population participate in job-related training, half the OECD average (40.4%). Although the low-skilled are arguably those who are in most need of training, only 9.5% of them train in Italy, less than half the OECD average (around 20%). Within this context, Italian firms could play a greater role in upskilling its workforce. The CVT Survey shows that in Italy, only 60.2% of firms (with at least 10 employees) provide continuous vocational training to their workers, lower than the OECD European average of 76.1%, a rate which places Italy at the bottom of the OECD ranking ahead only of Poland, Hungary and Greece (see Figure 1.5).

Figure 1.5. Adults' participation and firms' provision of training, Italy and OECD countries

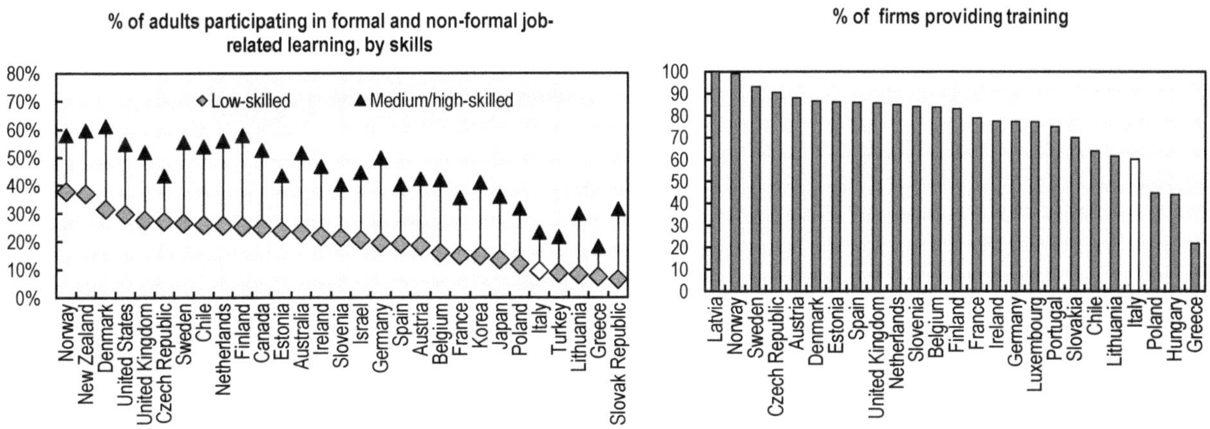

Note: for data on firms' provision of training, data for Chile refers to 2014, and 2016 for all other countries; the low-skilled refer to adults with low numeracy and literacy skills.
Source: data on adults' participation to training: PIAAC survey; data on firms' provision of training: CVTS; ENCLA for Chile; Basic Survey of Human Resource Development for Japan; Business Operations Survey for New Zealand.

Overall, while Italy has made major progress in the past decade to up-skill its population and workers, it is crucial that further efforts are put in place to improve access to good quality adult learning opportunities. Training Funds represent one very important tool through which Italy could face the pressures brought about by the mega-trends, and equip adults and workers with the skills needed to thrive in the labour market and society.

References

Nedelkoska, L. and G. Quintini (2018), "Automation, skills use and training", *OECD Social, Employment and Migration Working Papers*, No. 202, OECD Publishing, Paris, http://dx.doi.org/10.1787/2e2f4eea-en. [1]

OECD (2019), *Getting Skills Right: Future-Ready Adult Learning Systems*, OECD Publishing, Paris, https://doi.org/10.1787/25206125. [2]

Chapter 2. An overview of Training Funds

Training Funds (TFs) are associations run by social partners that finance workers' training, using resources collected through a training levy imposed on employers. Since their implementation, they have significantly encouraged firms to provide training to their workers, and positively influenced participation to adult learning opportunities. This chapter provides a brief description of the history of Training Funds, how they work, as well as recent developments in the legal framework that have modified the way Training Funds operate and function.

2.1. Brief history of Training Funds in Italy

Training Funds (hereafter TFs) are associations run by social partners that finance workers' training, using resources collected through a training levy imposed on employers. The main policy goal of the Training Funds is to provide incentives to firms to invest in the human capital of their workers and promote continuous learning and skills development opportunities.

Training Funds were instituted by law in 2000[1] by the Ministry of Labour and Social Affairs, following up on an initial provision set in the late 1990s',[2] and became operative in 2004.[3] The number of Training Funds has increased since their inception, passing from 10 as of 2004 to 19 Training Funds today.[4] Of the Training Funds that are operative today, 16 are exclusively devoted to (non-managerial) employees, and 3 to (employed) managers (Alessandrini, 2017[1]; 2017[2]).

Since their inception, Training Funds have rapidly increased their importance and outreach. From 2004 to 2017, the number of firms enrolled in a Training Fund has tripled and the number of workers covered by the scheme has doubled. Today Training Funds cover almost 1 million firms[5] and over 10 million workers, capturing almost the totality of potential adherents[6] (Casano et al., 2017[3]). In the Piedmont Region, for example, Training Funds cover 83% of firms[7] and 94% of dependent employees (SISFORM, 2017[4]). Managing EUR 603 million in 2017 (ANPAL, forthcoming[5]), Training Funds represent one of the most important sources for financing workers' continuous learning in Italy.

Training Funds have likely had a significant impact on the participation of Italian companies in continuous vocational training (OECD, 2014[6]). Before the introduction of the Training Funds, training often represented a marginal element in the strategies of companies, while today firms are much more likely to provide training than in the past (see Figure 1.4). The increase in the share of firms providing training to its employees was accompanied by an increase of 341% in the number of firms involved in Training Funds-sponsored training in the period 2008-2015 (Natili and Marcolin, 2017[7]).

2.2. How do Training Funds work?

One distinctive feature of Training Funds is that they are run by social partners. Training Funds' management boards comprise equal numbers of representatives appointed from employers and workers' organizations.[8] While Training Funds work autonomously, they function under the umbrella of government bodies. The Ministry of Labour and Social Affairs authorises the establishment of new Training Funds after verifying compliance with a set of requirements, and can temporarily suspend or terminate them if these requirements are no longer met. Since 2015[9], the National Agency for Active Labour Market Policies (ANPAL) is responsible for monitoring that the activities of the Training Funds are compliant with the rules.

Training Funds are financed through a levy-grant mechanism. Firms can allocate part of the 'mandatory contribution for involuntary unemployment' – 0.3% of workers' payroll, paid to the INPS (National Institute for Social Security) – to a Training Fund of their choosing. If a firm voluntarily joins a Training Fund, the INPS directly transfers the 0.3% to the selected Training Fund. Companies that do not elect to join a Training Fund still need to pay the 0.3%, which integrates government budgets and can be used to serve different purposes.

Enterprises can join only one of the 16 Training Funds for (non-managerial) employees at a time, and can additionally join one of the 3 Training Funds for (employed) managers (i.e. Fondir, Fondirigenti and Fondo Dirigenti PMI). On top of choosing which Training Fund(s) to enrol to, enterprises also chose the training provider that will deliver the course – although the training provider typically has to respect some minimum quality standards, e.g. they have to be accredited by the region, and/or by a Training Fund itself (see Chapter 5).

The amount of funding managed by each Training Fund depends on the number of employees covered and of the level of wages paid to them. Training Funds use the resources to finance training programmes at the firm, sectoral, or regional levels. They can also finance individual training programmes, through vouchers. All types of training programmes need to be agreed by social partners.

Training Funds finance training programmes through two channels: 1) Collective account (*conto collettivo*); and 2) Individual account (*conto formazione*). The characteristics of these financing channels are highlighted below:

- **Collective account** (*conto collettivo*): this account is directly managed by Training Funds and finances training through public calls (avvisi). Enterprises develop training plans (i.e. training proposals) and apply for funding, while Training Funds approve or reject the financing after a selection process. The collective account follows strategic logics, as public calls can be steered towards certain categories of workers (e.g. the low-skilled; women; older people) firms (e.g. SMEs) or skills (e.g. ICT; transversal skills).
- **Individual account** (*conto individuale*): this account can directly be used by firms to finance training projects for their own employees. Unlike collective accounts, individual accounts follow the logic of "mere restitution", whereby a share of each firm's contributions (generally 70%) paid to INPS is simply returned to the firm. This financing channel is typically used by larger firms, as smaller firms often do not accrue sufficient resources to finance workers' training.

2.3. Recent developments

In recent years, there have been several interventions by the government that have on the one hand reduced funding available to Training Funds, and on the other hand modified/updated the legal framework. These interventions have significantly modified the way Training Funds operate and function.

2.3.1. Resources available to Training Funds

In recent years, the government has diverted part of the funds normally destined to Training Funds for purposes other than training. As a result, since 2011, Training Funds have been able to access only a (decreasing) share of resources (see Figure 2.1). In 2017, out of the EUR 735 million collected by INPS through firms' payroll contributions, only 58.9% were effectively transferred to Training Funds. Several observers argue how, in practice, Training Funds today access only 0.19-0.2% of payroll paid by firms, rather than the 0.3% instituted by law.

Figure 2.1. Share of resources diverted from Training Funds

% of overall resources available from the 0.3% on payroll paid by firms (2011-2017)

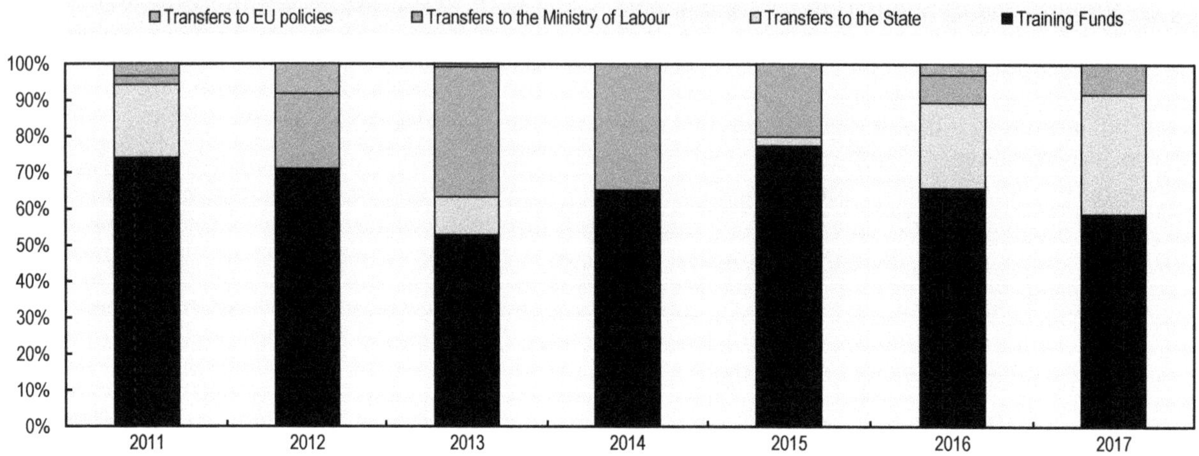

Note: Transfers to the State include: Art. 19 L. N. 2/2009; ex Art 254 L. N. 228/2012; Law N. 190/2014; Comma 284 and 294 of Law 208/15. Transfers to Ministry of Labour include: Fondo di Rotazione; CIG Deroga. Transfers to EU Policies include: Fondo Politiche Comunitarie.
Source: ANPAL ($2018_{[8]}$).

Funds were initially diverted on an exceptional basis to respond to the profound economic crisis. Indeed, from the first years of the crisis until 2015, parts of the Training Funds' resources were used to support welfare measures, for example to finance wage support measures for redundant workers (i.e. Income Redundancy Fund - Cassa integrazione guadagni, or CIG).

From 2015 onwards, however, government withdrawals have been made structural (ANPAL, $2018_{[8]}$). For example, the law 190/2014 establishes that starting from 2016 EUR 120 million per year shall be cut every year from Training Funds' budgets and absorbed into general government revenues. In addition, the 2015 Budget Law (208/15) establishes that for the years 2017 and 2018 part of the funds shall be used to finance subsidised part-time contracts (contratti di lavoro a tempo parziale agevolato) for older workers who wish to work part-time before reaching retirement age.[10]

While government withdrawals are common in countries with a levy-system in place (OECD, $2017_{[9]}$)[11], in Italy these curtailments are particularly worrying given that resources available to Training Funds are already limited by international standards. To give some examples, in France, the Organismes Paritaires Collecteurs Agréés (hereafter OPCA) manage around EUR 7 000 million, compared to only around EUR 600 million in Italy. In Ireland, Skillnet grants roughly EUR 240 per employee trained (ILO, $2017_{[10]}$), while in Italy Training Funds grants on average around EUR 184 per participant (ANPAL, $2018_{[8]}$).

Given the good coverage of firms by Training Funds, relatively low funding can be explained by the low contribution rate from which resources are drawn. The training levy rate in Italy (0.3% of payroll) is quite low compared to international standards. By way of example, contributions are equal to 0.8% in Ireland, up to 1% in France[12], 1.5% in Hungary, up to 2% in the Netherlands, and up to 2.5% in the UK (see Table 2.1). Some countries, like Ireland, are even planning to raise the levy-rate in the next years to further strengthen the adult learning system.[13] Moreover, unlike what happens in Italy, in some countries (e.g. the Netherlands; France) training funds' resources include, on top of employers' mandatory contributions, also employers' voluntary contributions, employers' sectoral contributions negotiated through collective agreements, government funding, and/or European funding.[14]

Table 2.1. Contribution rates of training levies in selected OECD and non-OECD countries

Country	Levy-rate (% of payroll)	Differentiation	Type
Australia	1.5%	No	Levy-exemption
Belgium	0.1% to 0.6%	By sector	Levy-exemption
Canada (Quebec)	1%	No*	Levy-exemption
Denmark	DKK 2 702 **	No	Revenue-generating/cost-reimbursement
France	0.55% to 1%	By firm size	Levy-grant
Greece	0.24%	No	Levy-exemption
Hungary	1.5%	No	Levy-exemption/revenue-generating/levy-grant
Ireland	0.8%	No	Ley-exemption/revenue-generating
Italy	0.3%	No	Levy-grant
Korea	0.1% to 0.7%	By firm size	Levy-grant
Netherlands	Up to 2%	By sector	Levy-grant
Poland	0.25%	No	Levy-grant
Spain	0.7% (of which 0.1% on workers)	No	Levy-exemption
United Kingdom	0.5% to 2.5%	By fund	Levy exemption
Non-OECD countries			
Brazil	1% to 1.5%	By firm size	Revenue-generating
South Africa	1%	No*	Levy-grant/revenue-generating

Note: **Canada (Quebec) and South Africa exempt the obligatory 1% of payroll contribution for firms with a payroll under a certain threshold. **Denmark has a lump sum of DKK 2 702 per full-time employee per year paid to the AUB, which reimburse wages paid to employees undergoing off-the-job training.
Source: Based on UNESCO (2018[11]), Müller and Behringer (2012[12]), OECD (2017[9]).

Curtailments in Training Funds resources are particularly worrying if considered in conjunction with parallel cuts in other public resources available for continuous learning. National funds for continuous vocational training (236/93 law and 53/00 law) administered by regions have recently been suspended.[15] The focus of the European Social Fund (ESF) has recently been reoriented from continuous learning towards policies to assist vulnerable groups mostly affected by the crisis (ANPAL, 2018[8]). Taken together, these cuts may constitute a major setback for continuous learning in Italy.

In a context of low participation to training among workers, a rapidly ageing population and high shares of workers with low skills (see Chapter 1), a reduction in resources available to invest in continuous learning is something that Italy can ill-afford.

Besides the direct short-term impact on the resources available for continuous learning, budget cuts may also have indirect long-term consequences. In the view of many stakeholders, they may affect Training Funds' credibility, undermine overall trust in the system, and ultimately discourage firms to join or remain enrolled in a TF.

Moreover, budget cuts – coupled with delays in payments by the INPS[16] – also made resources more unstable and insecure over time, reducing the ability of Training Funds to plan their training strategies and operate effectively.

Going forward, for Training Funds to operate successfully it will be important for them to be able to count on a steady flow of financial resources available through the training levy. This requires strong institutions backed by law, and a clear separation between Training Funds and other funds controlled by the government and other bodies (Müller and Behringer, 2012[12]).

An additional policy option is to increase the contribution rate of 0.3% of payroll, in line with rates already applied in many OECD countries. In order to limit labour costs – which are already high in Italy – the additional contribution rate could be made refundable. Alternatively, additional contributions (beyond the 0.3%) could be negotiated by social partners through collective bargaining, reflecting the fact that different sectors/industries face different training needs, and that the cost of such training may vary substantially across sectors/industries.

2.3.2. The Law on State Aids and Public Procurement Legislation

Since the establishment of Training Funds in 2003, there have been various debates in Italy regarding whether the funding they manage should be considered as public or private financial resources. This distinction is important in practical terms because it has implications on the way resources are administered by Training Funds, on Training Funds' autonomy on how to use the funds, as well as on the extent to which Training Funds are held accountable.

Indeed, the norms that originally established and regulated the activities of the Training Funds[17] were opaque around this point. Over the past decade, this legal vacuum has led to the proliferation of different (and sometimes contradicting) interpretations of the rules by public authorities – including the Constitutional Court, the Council of State, the National Anti-corruption Authority (ANAC), and the Italian Antitrust Authority (AGCM) – and overall uncertainty (Casano et al., 2017[3]).

In a view to put an end to these long-lasting debates and clarify the nature of the resources managed by the Training Funds, in 2016 the Ministry of Labour and Social Affairs, with a letter addressed to ANAC (Ministry of Labour and Social Affairs, 2016[13]), binds the funding managed by the Training Funds to the Law on State Aids[18] and Public Procurement Legislation. Following up on the Ministry's intervention, in 2018 ANPAL established a set of Guidelines that further clarifies the role and responsibility of Training Funds in light of these developments (see Section 2.3.3 and Annex A).

In practice, these developments bring two major changes in the way Training Funds operate: (i) all resources managed by Training Funds under the collective accounts fall under the Law on State Aids; and (ii) Training Funds have to purchase goods and services through competitive bidding processes, in respect of the Public Procurement Legislation and under the supervision of the ANAC.

These developments have several important implications for Training Funds. On the one hand, the new rules have helped increase accountability, and perhaps even pushed Training Funds to rethink their priorities and strategies. For example, the Law on State Aids puts limits in the way resources available in the collective account can be used – e.g. it forbids the financing of compulsory training (e.g. on health and safety) (see Section 4.7) – which has led many Training Funds to reorient their priorities and rethink their strategies.

On the other hand, however, many observers report how the new rules put additional administrative burdens on Training Funds – slowing down their activities and potentially hampering their ability to react quickly to the potentially rapid changes in the skill needs of firms.

Another concern is that Training Funds need to invest significant additional (financial and human) resources to make sure that they act in compliance with new regulation, possibly crowding out the resources available to finance workers' training.

All in all, with the new rules, Training Funds are not operating outside normal government budgetary channels anymore, a situation which has on the one hand enhanced accountability but also made Training Funds (similar to Regions) a much less flexible instrument.

2.3.3. ANPAL guidelines

On April 2018, ANPAL published the Guidelines for the management of resources attributed to TF ("*Linee Guida sulla gestione delle risorse finanziarie attribuite ai fondi paritetici interprofessionali per la formazione continua*") (hereafter, ANPAL Guidelines, or the Guidelines) (ANPAL, 2018[14]).

ANPAL Guidelines – developed in close collaboration with social partners – update an old (and arguably incomplete) legislation, and make sure that Training Funds can play by a clear, and shared, set of rules. In particular, they introduce some important novelties: they establish criteria for the use of funding; impose all Training Funds to establish a standardised internal regulatory framework; improve transparency and accountability; delineate the responsibilities of ANPAL; make the rules around "portability" stricter and clearer; and set the scene for the establishment of an integrated information system for adult learning (for a more detailed description of the Guidelines, see Annex A).

Overall, in the view of many stakeholders, the Guidelines represent a welcome and needed step in the right direction. They provide a much-needed update of the regulation and create a common understanding of what are Training Funds' roles and responsibilities.

Indeed, prior to the introduction of the Guidelines, the Training Funds have been operating in an opaque and uncertain legal framework: the law that set up the Training Funds (circolare 36/2003) was established over 15 years ago and, while it was originally conceived to only regulate the "start-up" period of the activities of the Training Funds, it was never updated (Casano et al., 2017[3]). So-designed, the original law – while providing significant margins of autonomy to Training Funds – perhaps provided insufficient details on how the JIFPs should operate.

The strategic objectives and the role of Training Funds have significantly evolved over time, too, – further highlighting the importance of updating the underlying legislation. Since the economic crisis, the potential outreach of Training Funds has expanded, shifting from the traditional target groups (the employed workers) and extending towards the unemployed and unemployed workers (cassa integrati) (see Section 6.2).

Moreover, the Guidelines reflect the recent developments in the legal framework, which has considerably changed the way Training Funds operate, by clarifying Training Funds' new obligations in the context of the Law of State Aids and Public Procurement Legislation (see Annex A).

Notes

[1] See Law 388/2000 and Law 289/2002.

[2] See Law 196/1997.

[3] See Law 289/2003.

[4] Since 2005 the Ministry of Labour and Social Affairs has approved the establishment of 12 new Training Funds. Three Training Funds were temporary suspended and then closed (Fo.in.coop; Fondazienda; FondAgri).

[5] Excluding firms in the agriculture sector.

[6] Potential adherents include all those firms that have at least one dependent employee.

[7] Excluding firms in the agriculture sector.

[8] Typically, the Training Funds' president is selected by the employers' representative organisations, while the vice-president is selected from the members of the workers' representative organisations.

[9] The Law n. 150 of September 4th 2015.

[10] The law 190/2014 establishes that starting from 2016, every year EUR 120 million are withdrawn from the 0.3%. The 2015 Budget Law (208/15) imposes that EUR 120 million for 2017 and EUR 60 million for 2018 are withdrawn from the 0.3% to finance the "contratti di lavoro a tempo parziale agevolato" to encourage older workers who are close to receiving old-age pension to continue working part-time.

[11] In Hungary, for example, employers complained that government uses resources to finance public training institutions, and more generally that it exercises too close control over the Fund, limiting its effectiveness. In Ireland, there was a very significant decline in the level of funding available to support training networks due to the recession in 2008 and 2009, both in terms of government funding support and co-investment from private enterprise.

[12] The levy is 0.55% for firms with less than 11 employees and 1% for larger firms.

[13] The Irish Government, as part of Budget 2018, decided to raise the rate of the National Training Fund levy by 0.1% in 2018 to 0.8% and by a further 0.1% in both 2019 and 2020.

[14] For example, in the Netherlands, most of O&O funding comes from national public finances and European subsidies – the European Social Fund (ESF).

[15] The Decree 150/2015 (and its subsequent amendments) has abolished two important Funds previously used by the Regions to finance education and training programs: (i) the Fund for Professional Training, established with Law 236/93, which was mainly used (though underutilised) to co-finance European Social Funds initiatives; and (ii) the resources made available with Law 53/2000, which mainly financed vouchers for individual training activities of workers.

[16] Many Training Funds lament that the INPS delays payments and it is very difficult for Training Funds to foresee the amount and time of payments.

[17] National Law 388/00; National Law 289/03; and Law 150/15.

[18] By definition, state aids are interventions (*e.g.* grants) issued by the State or through State resources, which give the recipient an advantage on a selective basis, and which can distort competition.

References

Alessandrini, G. (2017), *Atlante di Pedagogia del Lavoro (Pedagogy of Work Atlas)*, FrancoAngeli, Milano 2017. [2]

Alessandrini, G. (2017), *Nuovo Manuale per l'esperto dei processi formativi*, Carocci, Roma 2017. [1]

ANPAL (2018), *Linee Guida sulla gestione delle risorse finanziarie attribuite ai fondi paritetici interprofessionali per la formazione continua*, Agenzia per le politiche attive del lavoro. [14]

ANPAL (2018), "XVIII Rapporto sulla Formazione Continua", http://www.anpal.gov.it/Dati-e-pubblicazioni/Documents/XVIII-Rapporto-formazione-continua.pdf (accessed on 28 March 2018). [8]

ANPAL (forthcoming), *XIX Rapporto sulla Formazione Continua: Annualità 2017-2018.* [5]

Casano, L. et al. (2017), "Bilateralità e formazione", https://moodle.adaptland.it/mod/book/view.php?id=21892 (accessed on 7 February 2018). [3]

ILO (2017), "Upskilling SMEs", *International Labor Organization*, http://www.ilo.org/wcmsp5/groups/public/---ed_emp/---emp_ent/documents/publication/wcms_609267.pdf (accessed on 12 April 2018). [10]

Ministry of Labour and Social Affairs (2016), *Fondi Interprofessionali: Indicazione in materia di acquisizioni di beni servizi e contributi per le attività formative.* [13]

Müller, N. and F. Behringer (2012), "Subsidies and Levies as Policy Instruments to Encourage Employer-Provided Training", *OECD Education Working Papers*, No. 80, OECD Publishing, Paris, https://dx.doi.org/10.1787/5k97b083v1vb-en. [12]

Natili, M. and A. Marcolin (2017), "La formazione continua in Italia en in prospettiva comparata: dati e buone pratiche", *Centro di Ricerca e Documentazione Luigi Einaudi*, https://www.confindustriabergamo.it/files/assemblea/2017/centroeinaudi_confindustriabergamo_formazionecontinua.pdf (accessed on 6 February 2018). [7]

OECD (2017), *Financial Incentives for Steering Education and Training*, Getting Skills Right, OECD Publishing, Paris, http://dx.doi.org/10.1787/9789264272415-en. [9]

OECD (2014), *Italy: Key Issues and Policies*, OECD Studies on SMEs and Entrepreneurship, OECD Publishing, Paris, https://dx.doi.org/10.1787/9789264213951-en. [6]

SISFORM (2017), "Osservatorio Istruzione e Formazione Professionale: Piemonte 2017". [4]

UNESCO (2018), *Funding skills development: The private sector contribution*, http://unesdoc.unesco.org/images/0026/002619/261984e.pdf (accessed on 26 June 2018). [11]

Chapter 3. Increasing training participation and inclusiveness

A large and growing number of firms and workers are covered by Training Funds. However, certain firms (e.g. SMEs) may still face substantial barriers in adhering to/using the schemes, and training may not reach the most vulnerable workers (e.g. the low-skilled, older people). This Chapter looks at the barriers (e.g. administrative, time-related, financial) that can undermine the access to and use of Training Funds and highlights potential mechanisms to make the scheme more inclusive.

The statistical data for Israel are supplied by and under the responsibility of the relevant Israeli authorities. The use of such data by the OECD is without prejudice to the status of the Golan Heights, East Jerusalem and Israeli settlements in the West Bank under the terms of international law.

3.1. Encouraging SMEs to use Training Funds

Italian SMEs benefit less from the financial support available through the Training Funds than bigger firms. This section highlights the many obstacles – e.g. financial, informational, and administrative – that hamper their access to and use of TF-supported training.

3.1.1. SMEs are less likely to provide training to their workers

In Italy – like in other countries – smaller firms are less likely to provide training to their workers than larger firms. Data from the European Continuing Vocational Education Survey shows that training provision increases with firm size: 57.1% of small enterprises (with 10-49 employees) provide training to their workers, compared to 82% of medium-sized enterprises (with 50-249 employees) and 93.3% of large firms (250 employees or more).

While a similar pattern can be found in other countries, in Italy the gap in training provision between small and large firms is very high (36.2 percentage points),[1] the highest among OECD countries with available data, after Hungary (52.9), Greece (49.6), and Poland (46.9), and well above what can be observed in countries like Latvia and Norway where this gap is virtually inexistent (see Figure 3.1). This gap is particularly worrying considered that SMEs in Italy represent the vast majority of firms while larger firms (with 250 employees or more) represent only 0.08% of all enterprises (OECD, 2017[1]).

Figure 3.1. Enterprises (10 employees or more) providing training, by firm size, 2015

Percentage of all enterprises

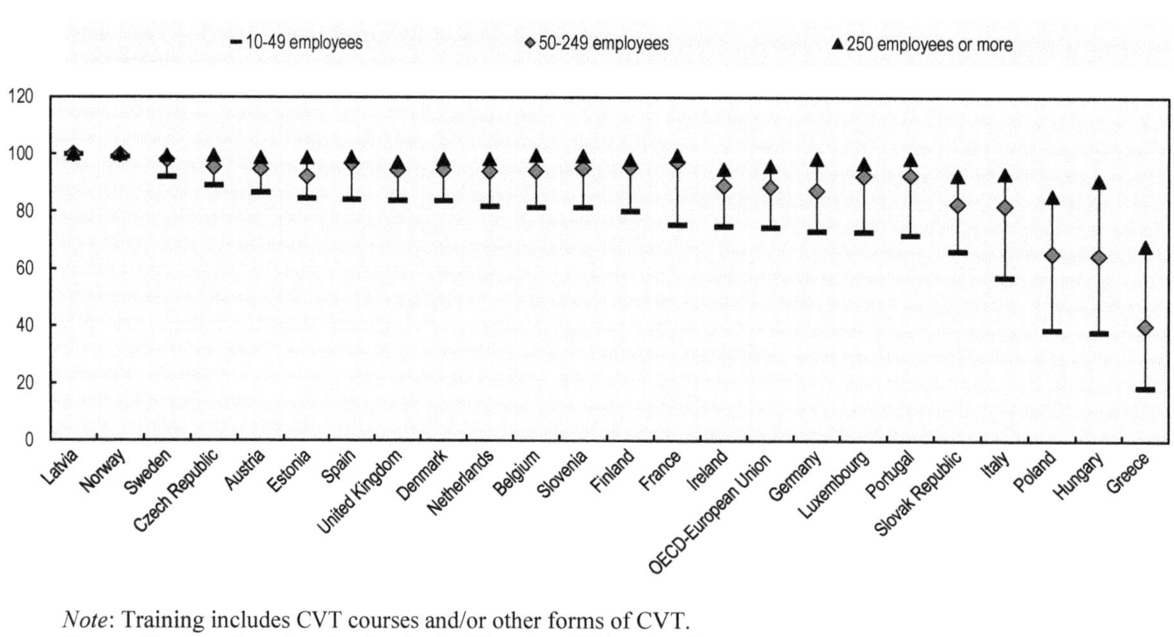

Note: Training includes CVT courses and/or other forms of CVT.
Source: Eurostat, based on the Continuing Vocational Education Survey.

3.1.2. SMEs less often receive financial support for training

Not only Italian SMEs train less their workers compared to larger firms, but also when they do train, they use funding support available (such as the one provided by the Training Funds) much less often than larger firms. Indeed, SMEs in Italy are typically less likely to use Training Funds funding and take up the opportunity to train their staff, while large companies often take the lion's share of training funds (Johanson, 2009[2]) (OECD, 2014[3]).

While on average SMEs represent the vast majority of all TF-supported firms – as of October 2017 83.4% of the supported firms had less than ten employees, 13.9% had 10 to 49 employees, and 2.3% had 50 to 249 employees, and 0.4% had 250 employees or more (ANPAL, 2018[4]) – these figures must be contrasted with the distribution of firm size in the population.

Indeed, ISTAT's elaborations of the Continuing Vocational Education Survey show that only 6.2% of small firms (10-19 employees) that provide training to their employees receive financial support from training funds, a share that evenly increases with firm size up to 64.1% for very large firms (with 1000 employees or more) (see Figure 3.2).

Worryingly, SMEs' lower use of financial support from Training Funds is not compensated by a more extensive use of other financing channels. Indeed, as shown in Figure 3.2, SMEs are also less likely to receive other types of financial support for training e.g. tax incentives, EU subsidies (e.g. European Social Fund), government subsidies, or other (private) sources.

Overall, SMEs seem to pay training using their own financial resources, probably due to a number of reasons, including: the lack of a sufficient number of employees to be eligible for funding; lack of information about the availability of Training Funds (and other public) funding; and administrative barriers to access to funding (see later sections for further details).

The under-representation of SMEs among recipients of Training Funds support represents a missed opportunity for Italian SMEs to tap on existing financial resources to expand workers' training and potentially improve their performance and competitiveness.

Moreover, the inequality in the uptake of JIFPs-supported training may effectively lead to a redistribution of resources from smaller to larger companies, and therefore may widen, rather than reduce, the divide between different-sized companies (UNESCO, 2018[5]).

Figure 3.2. Enterprises (10 employees or more) that received financial support to provide training, by firm size, Italy, 2015

% of enterprises that provided training

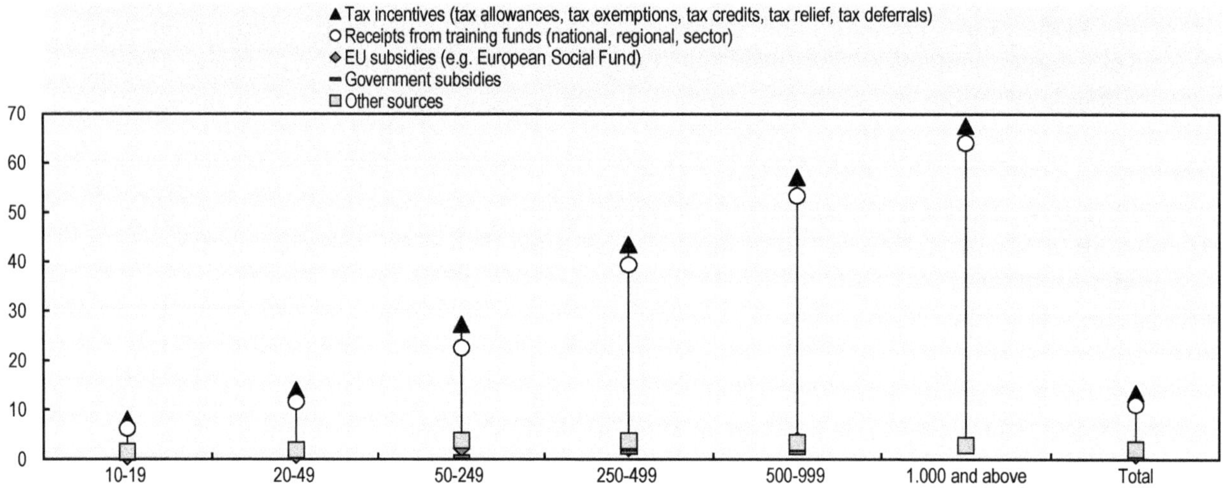

1. Percentages do not add up to 100% because multiple answers are possible.
2. "Other" refers to receipts from private foundations, receipts from external bodies/persons for the use of the enterprise's own training centre, receipts for training provision to external bodies/persons that are not part of the enterprise.
Source: Istat, based on the Continuing Vocational Education Survey 2015.

The under-representation of SMEs in levy-supported training schemes is a challenge that Italy shares with other countries. In Ireland, for example, only 3% of micro-firms (with less than 10 employees) participate in Skillsnet-supported training, compared to 79% among larger firms (with 50-249 employees) (ILO, 2017[6]). Similarly, sectoral training funds in Belgium and the Netherlands see a lower take-up of training by SMEs (OECD, 2017[7]; Eurofound, 2016[8]; Eurofound, 2016[9]).

Perhaps Italy could draw from the experience of OECD countries that have tried to address similar challenges in the past. Korea, for example, at the beginning of the years 2000s' implemented a comprehensive policy package specifically aimed at increasing the use of training levy schemes among SMEs, which has been very successful and is still running today (see Box 3.1).

Box 3.1. Increasing the use of Levy-Grant schemes among SMEs: The example of *SME Training Consortium* in Korea

In the mid-1990s, the Korean government introduced a training levy-grant scheme, to which all enterprises (including SMEs) were required to contribute as part of their unemployment insurance fees for their workers.

Despite the flexibility given to firms – e.g. firms had a great degree of autonomy to choose training providers, courses, and methods – the levy-grant system did not work properly for SMEs. Indeed, only 4.7% of SMEs offered levy-supported training to 4.2% of their workers, compared to 77.6% of large enterprises and 37.5% of workers.

This was considered as a serious policy issue, as SMEs accounted for 99.9% of the total enterprises and provided 86% of all contracted employment opportunities in the country. The scheme was considered to be inequitable, too, considered that although many SMEs paid the contributions to the levy, very few benefited in the end.

To address this challenge, in 2001 the Korean government piloted the *Training Consortium Pilot Program for SMEs* with the specific objective of removing (financial, organisation, technical) barriers to SMEs' use of the levy.

The pilot organised SMEs (within the same sectors/industries) into a Training Consortium (TC). Each TC set up an Operational Committee (OC), composed of various stakeholders such as member SMEs, local Chamber of Commerce and Industry, Ministry of Labour field office. The TC was managed and run by two training specialists, which were responsible for:

- conducting skills and training need assessment of each member SME (e.g. through interviews with SME managers and workers);
- planning training programme activities of member SMEs;
- contracting with training providers and SMEs to train their workers collectively;
- carrying out networking activities with TC members, through a web page, emails, and periodic meetings;
- carrying out evaluation studies upon completion of training courses.

The *Training Consortium Pilot Program for SMEs* considerably improved the use of the levy-grant scheme by SMEs: the proportion of member SMEs which offered training for their workers increased from 11% to 50% within a year of the pilot's implementation. The increase in the utilisation of the levy brought positive results on workers' productivity, and helped relieving skills shortages faced by SMEs. In addition, it helped in setting up a demand-driven training system, through the establishment of a strong partnership among stakeholders.

In 2003, the pilot was scaled up to the national level and today is considered as a successful flagship programme under the aegis of the Ministry of Labour.

Source: Lee and Sahu (2017[10]); Lee (2016[11]).

3.1.3. Further reducing the cost of training for SMEs

One reason for the lower uptake of Training Funds by SMEs may be linked to the direct cost of training. Typically, Training Funds cover only a share of the training cost (roughly 65% of total costs),[2] and SMEs (unlike larger firms) may find it difficult to pay for the difference.

Moreover, because Training Funds refund costs only after that training has taken place, many SMEs may face cash flow constraints that make it impossible for them to pay upfront the cost of training, especially if refunds take place after a long period of time.

Opportunity costs can also be high for SMEs. Employers (especially in SMEs) may find it challenging to continue paying workers' salary while they are on training, and replacing employees for the duration of the training may be difficult and expensive.

Another key challenge is that SMEs in general incur a higher training cost per worker compared to larger enterprises, because they have a smaller number of employees and thus cannot benefit from economies of scale.

Finally, Italian SMEs – unlike larger firms – are typically unable to use all Training Funds' financing channels available. While all SMEs can have access to collective accounts (by submitting training proposals to public calls), often they do not accrue sufficient savings in their individual account – whose resources are directly linked to firms' number of employees and their wages (see Section 2.2).

For example, data published by the largest TF, Fondimpresa, shows that among all participants to training activities financed through individual accounts, 43.7% are part of a very large firm (500 employees or more), while only 3.5% are workers from micro-firms (1-9 employees) (Fondimpresa, 2016[12]).This is despite the fact that micro-firms employ 45.9% of all Italian workforce (OECD, 2017[1]).

Table 3.1. Participants in *individual account*, Fondimpresa, 2016

Number and % of participants, by firm size

Firm size	Number of training participants	% of participants
1-9 employees	67 643	3.5%
10-49 employees	272 938	14%
50-99 employees	208 227	10.7%
100-249 employees	329 085	16.8%
250-499 employees	221 994	11.4%
500 employees or more	854 182	43.7%
Total	1 954 069	100%

Note: Participants are counted only once when they have participated to more than one training programme.
Source: Fondimpresa (2016[12]).

Training Funds have put forward several innovative practices to reduce the direct cost of training for SMEs. For instance, some Training Funds (e.g. *Fondimpresa*) can provide SMEs with additional financial resources (*contributo aggiuntivo*) when they are unable to finance training programmes solely through the individual account.

Several attempts are also being taken to help SMEs build economies of scale – although they could be expanded more broadly. For example, the SMEs network - *Associazione Piccole Imprese* (A.P.I.), brings together Italian SMEs so that they can pool employees into the same training programme, share the cost of training, and benefit from reduced costs through economies of scale. However, in the views of some stakeholders the awareness of SMEs of this approach is still limited (OECD, 2014[3]). Finally, over the past years, some Training Funds (e.g. Fonarcom) have adopted "aggregated" enterprise accounts into which several SMEs can pull resources together – however, recently the legal viability of these accounts has been questioned by ANPAL.[3]

Going forward, there are additional policy options that Italy could explore to reduce training costs for SMEs and ultimately increase take-up, building on the positive experience of countries that have been confronted with similar challenges:

- **Grant SMEs higher reimbursement rates, so as to reduce the direct cost of training for SMEs**. This is an approach that has already been implemented by some OECD countries with a levy scheme in place. In Poland, for instance, the National Training Fund[4] finances 80% of training costs for larger firms and 100% for micro-firms[5] (Eurofound, 2016[13]). In Korea, the training levy grants a higher refunding rate for SMEs, 270% of training levies paid, against 100% for larger firms.
- **Shorten/remove delays in reimbursements**. One policy option would be to have the TF pay for the training at the time of approval of the training plan, rather than through reimbursements. This would limit the financial constraints SMEs can face when advancing payments. This approach is adopted in Korea (Lee and Sahu, 2017[10]).
- **Reduce opportunity-costs of training**. One way to do that is to reimburse firms for workers' wages during training. For example, in Denmark, when an employee receives full wages while attending a course, the employer may apply for grants (e.g. state grant for adult training, VEU godtgørelse)[6] or in some cases receive top-ups from training funds to cover workers' wages. Similar top-up mechanisms are also being implemented by some training funds in the Netherlands (OECD, 2017[14]). Another way to reduce opportunity-costs is through job rotation schemes, whereby firms are given support to find a temporary replacement worker (e.g. usually an unemployed person) during the training period. These schemes today can be found in some OECD countries (Denmark, Finland) (OECD, 2017[15]; OECD, 2019[16]).
- **Exempt, or reduce, contributions paid by SMEs**. Some countries have adopted this strategy to encourage SMEs to take up training levy schemes more extensively. In France, training levies are 0.55% for firms with less than 10 employees, and 1% for larger firms. In Malaysia, the Human Resource Development Fund (HRDF) levy scheme applies a payroll levy of 0.5% for SMEs (with less than 50 employees) and 1% for larger firms (Ziderman, 2016[17]). In Brazil, the National Industrial Apprenticeship Service (SENAI)[7] imposes a 1% payroll levy on all industrial enterprises and 1.5% for large companies (more than 500 employees) (see Table 2.1).

3.1.4. Fostering a learning culture among SMEs through entrepreneurs' training

But further reducing the cost of training, alone, will likely not suffice to raise the use of Training Funds by SMEs. According to several stakeholders, what is also limiting the full use of Training Funds is the lack of a learning culture among Italian SMEs.

There may be several underling reasons. One relates to Italian SMEs' low demand for skills. The productive structure of the Italian economy is characterised by many small, family-led, businesses, which are often concentrated in traditional sectors. These businesses often employ low-skilled workers and produce low value-added goods, and therefore may see little value in workers' training (OECD, 2017[18]; OECD, 2017[19]).

There is also little awareness of the benefits of training among Italian SMEs. Because systematic impact evaluation of (TF-supported-) training is scant in Italy, many SMEs may not be fully convinced about the benefits of continuous training, for example on firms' performance.

Negative perceptions of training quality may be another issue. According to several stakeholders, there seems to be a general perception that sponsored-training is often of poor quality and as such not very useful.

All in all, it seems that fostering a learning culture among Italian SMEs will partly rely upon efforts to shift the Italian productive system towards the use of new and high value-added technologies (*e.g.* through industrial policies - see Section 4.7), nurture an impact evaluation culture and improve training quality (see Chapter 5).

On top of these efforts, changing entrepreneurs' attitudes towards training – *e.g.* through their own continuous upskilling – seems like another important step towards a more extensive use of Training Funds. Indeed, entrepreneurs are those who ultimately decide on firms' training strategies, especially in SMEs, and influencing their approach towards training could translate into better learning opportunities for staff. On the one hand, training content could specifically focus on human resources management practices and the importance of providing learning opportunities to employees. On the other hand, participation to training (even if not specifically focussed on HR management practices) could indirectly foster a learning culture among entrepreneurs.

While promising initiatives have been undertaken in Italy to promote entrepreneurship training, their outreach is limited, and mainly focused on young people (through initial education) or jobseekers (through the PES) (OECD, 2014[3]) – with little continuing training opportunities for established entrepreneurs.

One key challenge is that entrepreneurs cannot benefit from TF-supported training opportunities, as by law Training Funds can solely target *dependent* staff (whether non-managerial employees or employed managers) for whom firms pay the contribution of 0.3% on payroll (see Section 2.2).

In this context, one policy option worth exploring would be to encourage Training Funds to finance entrepreneurs' training, through additional contributions – alongside what has already been done on ad-hoc cases by certain Training Funds. For example, the Training Fund FAPI has recently allowed entrepreneurs of micro-firms to participate in training through the payment of additional contributions (Fondo Formazione PMI, 2017[20]). Similarly, in 2010 and 2012, *Fondo Formazienda* and the Lombardy Region have promoted joint grants, which included entrepreneurs as beneficiaries.

Alternatively, the government could provide additional funding to cover entrepreneurship training, similarly to what is already being done in some OECD countries. In Finland, for example, the Education Fund uses contributions from the State to finance the entrepreneurs' adult education allowance.

3.1.5. Raising awareness about financial opportunities available through Training Funds

One key challenge to a more extensive use of Training Funds among SMEs is that there is a general lack of awareness of the public support for workforce training (OECD, 2014[3]), and still too many Italian firms – especially SMEs – are not aware of the existence of Training Funds.

In Italy, several actors – including the government, social partners, Training Funds – could take responsibility for making Training Funds more widely known. The government could lead broad information awareness campaigns to raise awareness among SMEs on the benefits of continuous learning, and within this context promote the various financial support mechanisms available for training, including support available through Training Funds. Social partners, too, could do more to disseminate information among their members about funding opportunities available through Training Funds, leveraging their existing networks. And while each TF has its own outreach strategy, more can be done. For example, regional branches of the Training Funds could be expanded[8] to reach out to smaller firms located in remote areas, although this expansion would probably result in higher administration costs. Alternatively, in a view to contain costs, Training Funds could strengthen their links with existing organisations/associations (*e.g.* trade associations – *associazioni di categoria*) to promote their activities further.

But having more SMEs enrol in a TF will not be enough. Even member firms sometimes are not aware of being registered in a TF and therefore do not use the funding they are entitled to receive (Casano et al., 2017[21]). Indeed, evidence shows that only around 6% of the associated enterprises actually receive support for training programmes (Müller and Behringer, 2012[22]).

Further efforts need to be undertaken to promote the use of Training Funds among member firms, drawing from what has already been done by some Training Funds. For instance, *Fondimpresa*, sometimes restricts funding to training plans that include a certain share of firms that have never benefited from Training Funds-funding before. *Foncoop* uses regional branches to reach out to firms that are enrolled to Training Funds but do not use funding.

The lack of awareness among SMEs about training funds opportunities is a challenge that Italy shares with other countries: in Hungary, for example, some employers do not make full use of the possibilities offered by the training levy as they are not aware of them (Kis et al., 2008[23]); in Poland over 55% of firms have no knowledge about training funds and only 4.3% use them (Eurofound, 2016[13]). However, there are international good practice examples that Italy could learn from. For instance, Ireland has developed the *Irish Government's Supporting SMEs campaign,* which aims at increasing awareness of the range of Government supports available for start-ups and small businesses. In the context of this campaign, the government has developed an online guide ("Supporting SMEs Online Tool") conceived to help Irish start-ups and small businesses navigate the range of Government supports – including financing possibilities offered by the training levy scheme (i.e. *Skillnet Ireland*).

3.1.6. Reducing administrative procedures and red tape

Administrative requirements and red tape may be another key barrier to the utilisation of TF funding by SMEs. Unlike larger firms, SMEs often do not have a department exclusively devoted to planning, organising, and managing staffs' training – and thus they may find it difficult to cope with grant application procedures.

Indeed, data from the Continuous Vocational Training Survey show that in Italy 38.2% of firms with 10-49 employees have a specific person or unit responsible for organising CVT or have a training plan or budget including CVT, compared to 67.7% in firms with 50-249 employees and 87.9% in firms with 250 employees or more.

Moreover, SMEs may find it challenging to assess the training needs of their workers and tend to be discouraged more easily by a burdensome application process without knowing whether their application will be successful or not (OECD, 2014[3]).

Training Funds have already taken significant steps to reduce red tape and simplify firms' procedures to access funding. In a view to attract more firms, in fact, virtually all Training Funds have moved towards keeping paperwork at a minimum (see Section 5.3).

However, in the future, more could be done. As pointed out in a recent OECD report on SMEs in Italy, in order to minimise red tape, Training Funds could implement a simplified application procedure for SMEs, which would require firms to describe their training needs and the expected training outcomes (rather than designing a detailed training plan). The detailed training needs analysis and specification of the training contents could then be assigned to specialised trainers, who would take this burden away from the SMEs (OECD, 2014[3]).

3.2. Encouraging vulnerable workers to participate in training

As in other countries, in Italy vulnerable employees (e.g. the low-skilled; older workers) generally benefit less from training opportunities, often because employers tend to train those employees who are most likely to succeed and turn the skills gained into company profits (OECD, forthcoming[24]). Encouraging vulnerable workers to have access to TFs-supported training opportunities is crucial to ensure that training opportunities are available to all and that no one is left behind.

3.2.1. Vulnerable groups typically remain excluded from training opportunities

In Italy, the incidence of adults' participation in training varies considerably depending on socio-demographic and employment characteristics, with important inequalities in access to learning opportunities. While vulnerable groups struggle to participate in adult learning in all OECD countries, they seem to be particularly lagging behind in Italy.

Looking at socio-demographic characteristics, older people, women, lower-skilled and low-wage workers in Italy are less likely to take part in adult learning, when compared to both more advantaged groups in Italy and similar vulnerable groups in other OECD countries. Elaborations of the PIAAC Survey (see Figure 3.3), show that:

- Only 8.3% of older people (55 and over) participate in training compared to 23.9% of the prime age population (25-54). This places Italy at the bottom of the OECD distribution, with older people performing worse only in Greece and Turkey.
- Among women, 17.3% participate in training compared to 23% among men. Italian women participate much less in training compared to women in other OECD countries, with the only exception of Greece and Turkey.
- The low-skilled (*i.e.* with low literacy and/or numeracy skills) in Italy are much less likely to participate in training than more skilled people.[9] They also tend to

participate much less than peers in other countries, with only low-skilled in Greece, Lithuania, Slovak Republic and Turkey performing less well.

- Only 14.2% of low-wage workers (*i.e.* those earning less than two third of median wages) participate in training compared to 33.5% of higher-wages employees. This places Italy at the very bottom of the OECD distribution.

When analysing participation rates by employment characteristics, it appears that in Italy the unemployed, the long-term unemployed, temporary workers, and workers in SMEs are less likely to take part in adult learning, when compared to both more advantaged groups in Italy and similar vulnerable groups in other OECD countries. Indeed, elaborations of the PIAAC Survey (see Figure 3.4), show that:

- In Italy, only 10.7% of the unemployed population participate in training compared to 28.5% of the employed. Across OECD countries, only the unemployed in Lithuania and the Slovak Republic participate less.
- The long-term unemployed are particularly lagging behind: only 5.4% of them participate to training, the lowest share in the OECD and almost five times less than the OECD average of 24.3%.
- Large differences exist among employed people as well, and particularly between workers in temporary and permanent contracts. Indeed, only 21% of temporary workers in Italy participate to training, compared to 32% of permanent workers – a share that is lower than any other OECD country (OECD average 49.8%).
- Participation to training differs also depending on the size of the firm: only 27% of workers in SMEs participate to training, compared to 39.6% of workers in larger firms. Again, Italy performs much worse than the OECD countries considered, with the only exception of Turkey.

3.2.2. There are several barriers to training participation

Many adults in Italy are not willing to train. The analysis of the Survey of Adult Skills (PIAAC) suggests that 67% of adults did not participate and did not want to participate in adult learning activities in the year preceding the survey – the highest share in the OECD after Greece and Turkey and well above the average of 43% (see Figure 3.5).

One explanation for the lack of willingness to train might be that some adults in Italy are not sufficiently aware of the need for training or convinced of its effectiveness, returns and impact on career progression opportunities.

Another possible explanation relates to poor wage progression prospects, which is particularly relevant in a country like Italy where wage increases are more linked to seniority than productivity (OECD, 2017[19]). Recent research, in fact, shows that wage returns to adult learning are quite disappointing in Italy compared to other OECD countries with available data (Fialho, Quintini and Vandeweyer, forthcoming[25]).

Even those adults who are willing to train in principle face several obstacles to participation – that relate to time, financial and course availability constraints. According to PIAAC data for Italy, being too busy at work is by far the most frequently cited barrier to learning, reported by 40% of potential learners, followed by childcare or family responsibilities (19%), cost of training (15%), the fact that the course or programme is offered at an inconvenient place or time (5%), lack of employer's support (3%), and lack of pre-requisites (3%) (Figure 3.5).

Overall, this evidence suggests that Italy needs to strengthen policies to motivate adults to train – including policies that better link wage progression to productivity, along the lines of the recently implemented "*contratti di produttività*" (OECD, 2017[19]) – and implement measures aimed at removing barriers to participation for adults who are willing to participate in principle.

Figure 3.3. Gap in participation by socio-demographic characteristics

% of adults participating in formal and non-formal job-related learning

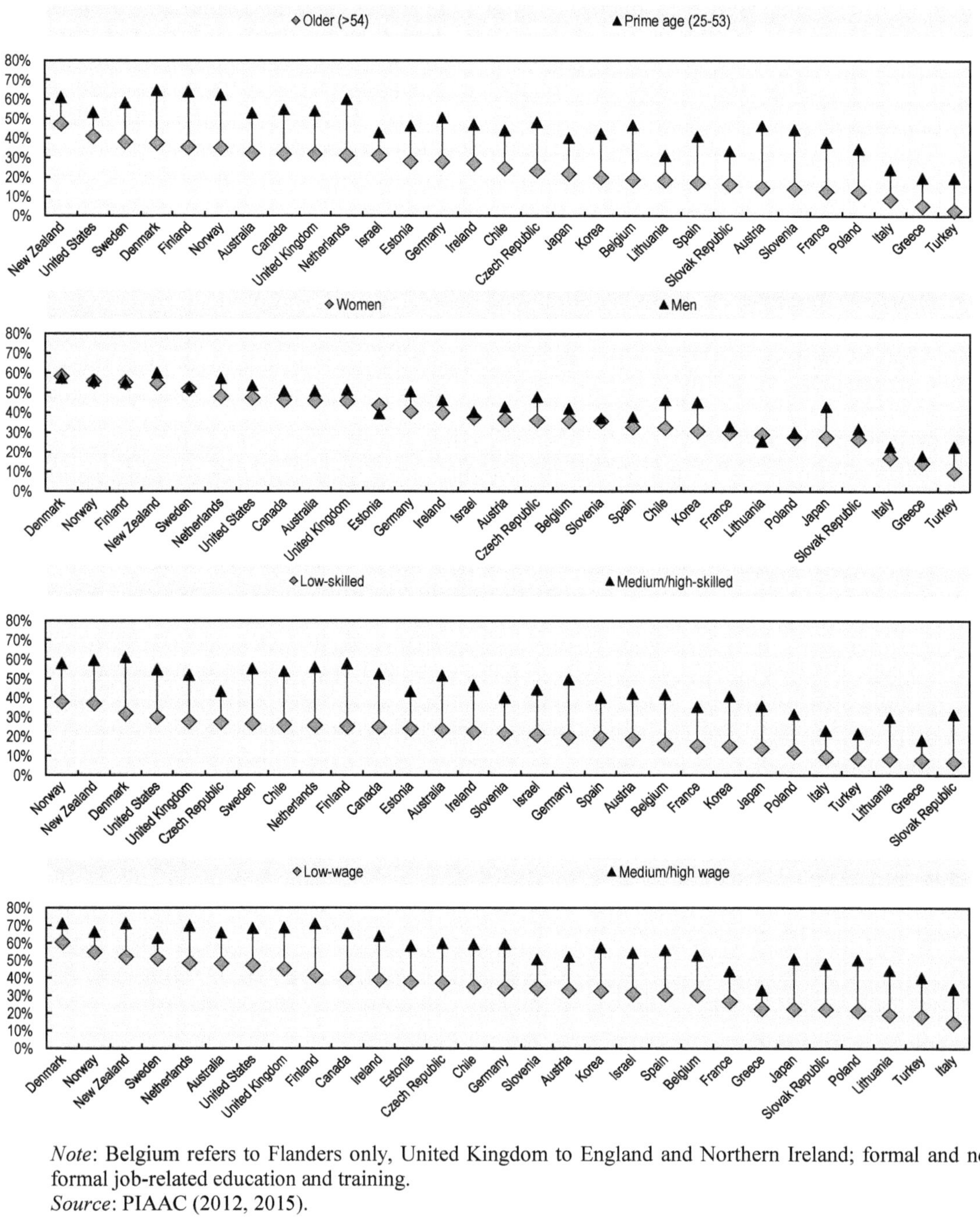

Note: Belgium refers to Flanders only, United Kingdom to England and Northern Ireland; formal and non-formal job-related education and training.
Source: PIAAC (2012, 2015).

Figure 3.4. Gap in participation by employment situation

% of adults participating in formal and non-formal job-related learning

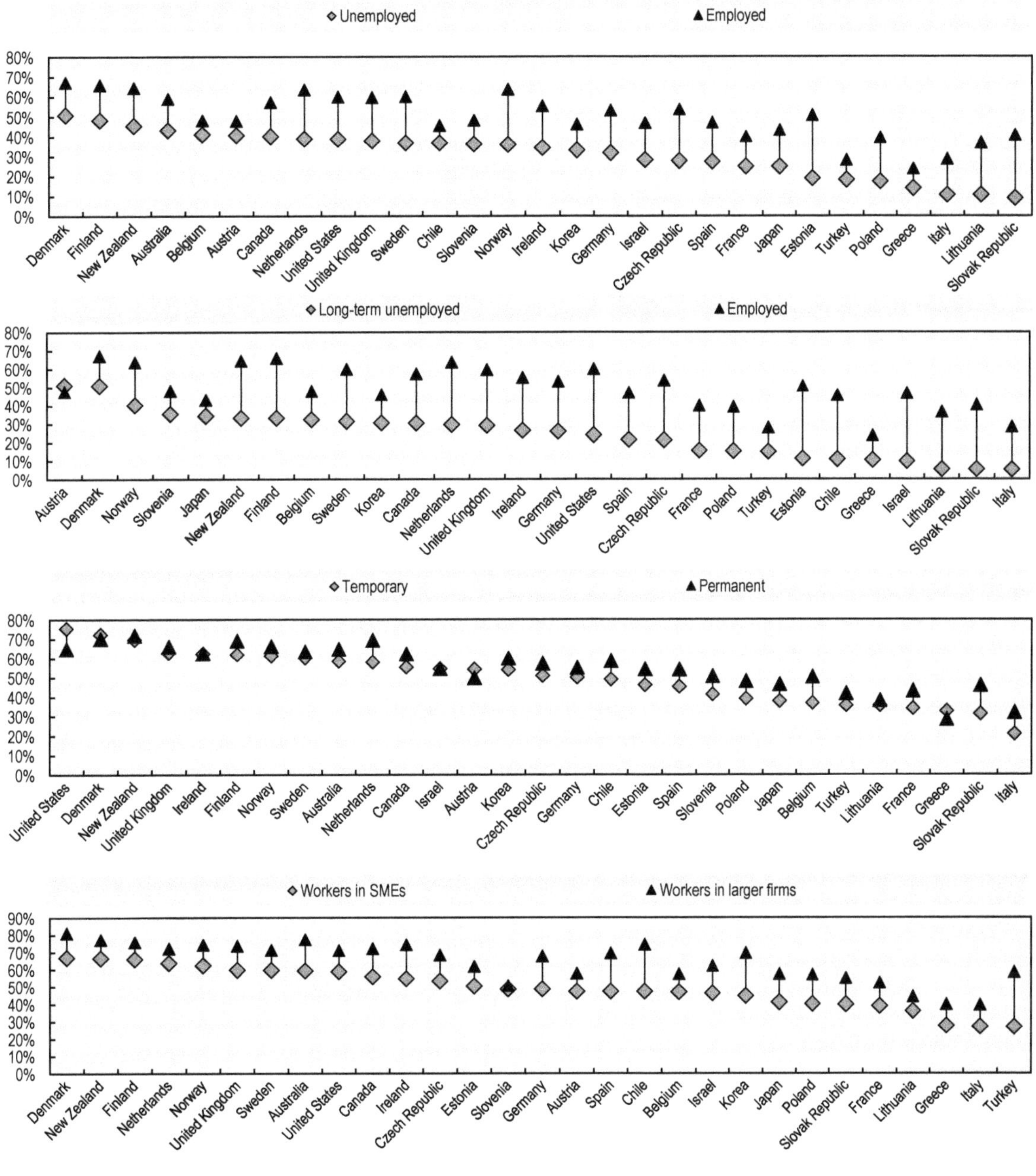

Note: Belgium refers to Flanders only, United Kingdom to England and Northern Ireland; formal and non-formal job-related education and training.
Source: PIAAC (2012, 2015).

Figure 3.5. Barriers to participation in training

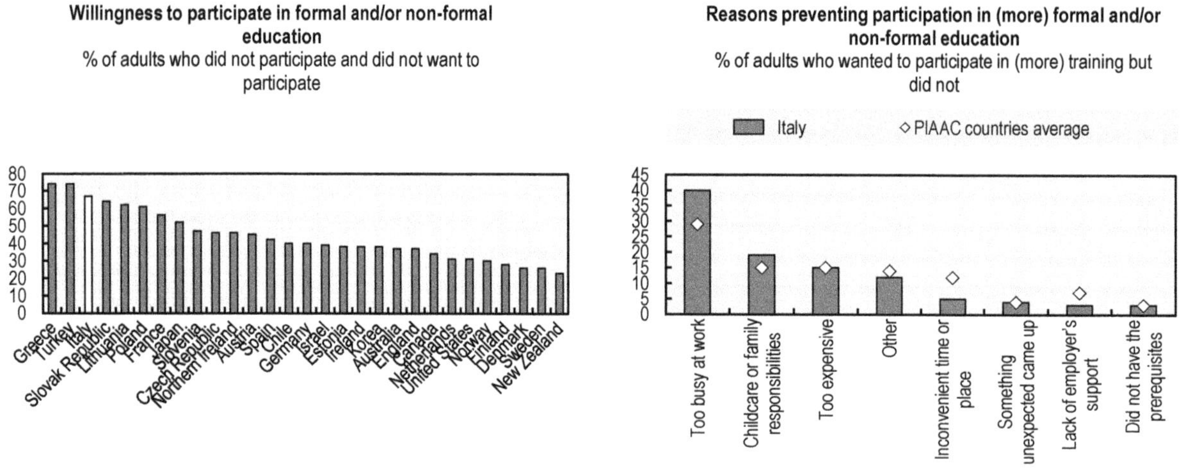

Source: OECD stat.

3.2.3. What is the role of Training Funds in ensuring that the most vulnerable are trained?

In Italy – like in other countries with a levy scheme in place – there is an open debate on whether (and to what extent) the low participation of vulnerable groups in training should be dealt with by Training Funds or with via other instruments of public nature (e.g. European Social Fund).

Considered that the levy is entirely financed through employers' contributions, there is a certain resistance (from employers) in excessively limiting or steering firms' decisions on the use of funds. Moreover, targeting support in favour of particular workers may generate substitution effects (*i.e.* between subsidised- and non-subsidised training participants).

The experience of OECD and emerging countries shows that the training levies' design plays a key role in whether they benefit the most disadvantaged. In some countries (*e.g.* Spain, the Netherlands), training levies are not specifically designed to be inclusive and often the most vulnerable are the least likely to benefit.[10] Conversely, in some countries (*e.g.* Singapore, South Africa) training levy funds are conceived to explicitly target disadvantaged groups.[11]

In Italy, while in principle Training Funds have potentially a big role to play to ensure that training efforts are focused on those groups of workers who would otherwise receive little training, in practice firms have a great deal of autonomy to decide what workers to train.[12]

While whether Training Funds should explicitly target vulnerable workers remains an issue of open debate, what is certain is that Training Funds should not exacerbate existing inequalities in training opportunities, or decrease skills financing for the most vulnerable relative to others.

Going forward, Training Funds could focus their efforts on ensuring that at least part of the funding is used to train vulnerable workers. For instance, trade unions could help monitoring the targeting of training programmes with an eye to the access of vulnerable groups. As another example, when using the *collective accounts*, Training Funds could give priority access to, or develop specific grants for, vulnerable groups, alongside what has already been done in ad-hoc cases by some of the Training Funds.[13] Shifting the responsibility to train from employers to individuals (*e.g.* by using individual training plans more broadly) (see Section 3.2.4), and adopting more flexible training delivery methods (see Section 3.2.5) are other policy options that Training Funds could look at going forward.

Of course, there is only so much that Training Funds can do to ensure that nobody is left behind, and complementary policies need to be strengthened/put in place by the government too. For instance, policies aimed at removing workers' barriers to training (*e.g.* education and training leave; financial incentives for workers to take-up training), additional measures that shift the responsibility of training away from firms and towards workers (*e.g.* through Individual Training Accounts; or individual rights to training), together with effective coordination mechanisms with other actors involved in adult learning[14] (see Chapter 6) are also crucial.

Good initiatives of this type are already being implemented in Italy. For example, according to a recent collective agreement, starting from January 2017 all firms in the metalwork industry have to provide 24 hours of training to each worker, every three years. In the absence of training, the worker has the right to participate to external training activities, for which two-thirds of spending should be borne by the firm for a maximum of EUR 300. This is a step in the right direction, although it is still too early to assess the effectiveness of the measure.

While these policies typically fall outside the responsibility of Training Funds – and are beyond the scope of this report – they can play an important role in ensuring that Training Funds reach vulnerable adults.

3.2.4. Using individual training plans more broadly

Shifting the responsibility to train from employers to individuals is one way to ensure that the most vulnerable have access to (TF-supported) training opportunities. Individual training plans can, at least in principle, help achieve this objective by targeting financing to workers at risk.

In Italy, individual training plans are one of the four financing channels through which firms can have access to TF funding (see Section 2.2). They are often financed through a voucher given to firms to sponsor individual workers' training.

Much like the other financing channels, individual training plans can be accessed through public calls, and therefore Training Funds have room to target them to certain categories of workers (including the disadvantaged).

Despite their potential to address the specific needs of vulnerable workers, however, individual training plans are the least frequently used type of TF-supported training, involving only 8.9% of firms and 1.6% of participants (see Table 3.2). One reason behind the low use of this financing channel may be that the content of training, being associated to the needs of specific individuals, may end up being very fragmented and therefore costly.

Table 3.2. Types of TF-supported training, 2016

Firms and participants benefiting from TF-supported training

	Number of firms	% of firms	Number of participants	% of participants
Firm	33 497	49.0	1 358 590	87.1
Individual	**6 110**	**8.9**	**24 909**	**1.6**
Sectoral	16 756	24.5	72 777	4.7
Territorial	12 052	17.6	104 120	6.7
Total	68 415	100.0	1 560 396	100.0

Note: The table includes training plans approved by TF from January to December 2016.
Source:. ANPAL (2018[4]).

Moreover, this instrument is rarely used to support the training of vulnerable workers. Firms typically decide how to spend the voucher (including on which beneficiaries), and they often use it for employees in senior positions, or to address specific needs of micro-firms (ANPAL, 2018[4]). In order to reach the most vulnerable, individual training plans need to be accessed on workers' demand without intermediation by the firm. So-designed, individual training plans may have the potential to empower vulnerable groups who would otherwise not receive any training by firms.

On top of using individual training plans more broadly and targeting them to the most vulnerable, Training Funds also need to assist workers to make the right skills decisions. For example, vouchers would need to be accompanied with skills assessments procedures to shed light on workers' skills gaps, guidance services to orient workers towards good quality training opportunities (and possibly training that brings highest wage returns), and skills certification procedures to increase workers' motivation to participate (see Section 5.2). These complementary support measures are particularly important for certain category of vulnerable people (e.g. older workers) who are less aware of the importance of training and less likely to spontaneously seek learning opportunities.

Going forward, Training Funds could grant a certain percentage of funding to individual training plans, while in parallel tight them to the most vulnerable and further invest in support measures (e.g. skills assessment; guidance; certification) to ensure high take-up.

Some Training Funds have already taken good steps in this direction. For example, the TF for temporary agency workers (*i.e.* Forma.Temp) has developed an effective training voucher system. The beneficiary of the voucher[15] has the right to a maximum of EUR 5 000 worth of training delivered by pre-identified training providers.[16] Interested candidates can directly apply for the voucher – without intermediation of the firm or the temporary agency – and can receive guidance and information support (*e.g.* on training opportunities available) by local Training Funds branches or through a dedicated electronic platform (www.form-and-go.it).

Going forward, the challenge for Italy will be to ensure that other Training Funds implement such a training voucher system, building on the experience of Forma.Temp. Italy could perhaps learn from what is happening in the Netherlands, where the government has already recognised the need to shift the responsibility for training from employers to individuals as a key skills policy priority. Similarly to what Forma.Temp is doing in Italy, in the Netherlands STOOF, the training fund devoted to temporary agency workers, has put in place a schooling voucher (EUR 500) which employees can directly access, without intermediation by the firm. The interesting aspect of the Dutch example is that other training funds in the Netherlands are also trying to adopt the schooling voucher system on a pilot basis, building on the experience of STOOF.

3.2.5. Adopting more flexible training delivery methods

Traditional training delivery methods (e.g. classrooms) may be ill-suited for adult workers, who have different needs compared to young people in initial education. Providing flexible learning opportunities (e.g. through e-learning), that are compatible with individuals' private and working lives, can help adult workers to combine their work and family responsibilities with education and training. Flexible learning opportunities can be particularly helpful for the most vulnerable, such as those working in remote areas (e.g. where training providers are scant) and for certain categories of workers who may need flexible training arrangements to be able to participate in training (e.g. parents of young children).

Italy seems to do better than other countries in the delivery of e-learning programmes. Elaborations of PIAAC show that 24.7% of individuals state that at least one of their (job-related) learning activity (in the past 12 months) was organised as distance learning, against 19.4% on average among PIAAC-participating countries.

Similarly, in Italy distance or time constraints seem to be less of a barrier to training participation. Only 5.3% of individuals wanted to participate in (further) training but did not for time or distance constraints, compared to an average of 11.9% for PIAAC-participating countries (see Figure 3.5).

Despite this positive picture, there is room for Training Funds to support e-learning more proactively. Indeed, the classroom remains the most frequently used type of TF-supported training, representing 77.5% of participants. 11.8% of participants take part in e-learning programmes, and the remaining participate in other types of flexible learning such as on-the-job training, workshops, job rotation or job shadowing (ANPAL, 2018[4]) (see Table 3.3).

Table 3.3. Types of TF-supported training delivery methods

	% of participants to TF-supported training
Classroom	**77.5%**
E-learning	11.8%
On-the-job training	5.8%
Job rotation or job shadowing	2.6%
Seminars or workshops	1.2%
Self-learning groups	1%
Total	100%

1. Data includes programmes approved in 2015 and started in 2016.
2. The question provides multiple answer choices. Therefore the sum of the answers is higher than the total of programmes approved. For the calculation of "% of training programmes" the sum of the individual answers is used.
Source: (ANPAL, 2018[4]).

In the views of many stakeholders, one of the reasons as to why TF-supported training is often delivered in classrooms is that this training delivery method is often easier to organise and monitor (*e.g.* through spot inspections). At the moment, different stakeholders claim that Training Funds are ill-equipped to monitor training that is delivered in more innovative manners, e.g. through e-learning, job rotation or job shadowing. In order to use more innovative learning methods further, Training Funds need to be adequately equipped to monitor and evaluate the successful delivery of all programmes, including e-learning (*e.g.* through – *ex-ante*, *in itinere* and *ex-post* examinations to test the competences acquired; and/or through skills certification).

Another key challenge of expanding e-learning opportunities is that some adults – e.g. those with low skills – may find it difficult to access more digitalised training programmes. Indeed, elaborations of PIAAC data seem to suggest that these adults are less likely to use e-learning than other population groups.[17] In order to improve access to online learning, and avoid that vulnerable groups remain excluded, it is important to ensure that adults are equipped with adequate ICT skills to start with.

Notes

[1] The gap refers to the gap between the percentages of small firms that provide training, compared to percentages of large firms that provide training.

[2] The average training cost of training plans concluded in 2016 was EUR 284 per participant, of which EUR 184 paid by an TF and the remaining EUR 100 paid by the firm. See ANPAL (2018[4]).

[3] These are accounts into which several firms (generally SMEs) pull resources to be able to accrue sufficient funds to finance workers' training. Although they can be designed in different ways, typically one leading firm is appointed by the TF to represent the interests of associated firms and can decide how to allocate resources. These "aggregated" enterprise accounts were originally conceived by FonARcom as an instrument to give SMEs further access to financing – but have subsequently been implemented by several Training Funds.

[4] *Krajowy Fundusz Szkoleniowy*

[5] With a cap of 300% of average wage per employee.

[6] In 2016 it was equal to around EUR 450 per week, or 80% of the maximum unemployment insurance benefit rate

[7] A sectoral training agency managed by the employer-side (National Confederation of Industry)

[8] Of the 19 Training Funds (excluding Forma.Temp) that are currently active today, only 6 have operational regional branches.

[9] The low-skilled refer to those who scored at or below level 1 in literacy and numeracy in the PIAAC survey. These are compared to all those people who scored at level 2 or above.

[10] For example, the training levy in Spain is found to be mainly used to support the training of male, middle-aged, and qualified employees; and sectoral training funds in the Netherlands may also suffer from these problems as only few funds are targeted to the vulnerable (Müller and Behringer, 2012[22]).

[11] In South Africa, for example, the policy objective of the training levy is that 85% of the training programmes should benefit blacks, 54% women, and 4% the disabled (OECD, forthcoming[24]; Johanson, 2009[2]). In Singapore, the Skills Development Fund was designed to actively target lower-income workers, undereducated individuals, and small and medium-sized enterprises (SMEs) (UNESCO, 2018[5]).

[12] Reliable data on participation to TF-supported training by individual characteristics is not available (see Chapter 5), and therefore it is difficult to assess with precision to what extent Training Funds funding are channelled towards the most vulnerable workers.

[13] Fondartigianato, for example, has already granted priority access to funding to youth (under 29) and women (Fondartigianato, 2012[26]).

[14] *E.g.* training financed by regions, training programmes for low-skilled adults provided by *Centri Provinciali per l'Istruzione degli Adulti* (CPIA), and training for the unemployed provided by the Public Employment Service.

[15] Beneficiaries need to be temporary agency workers, or unemployed people who have recently been temporary agency workers.

[16] The list includes training providers accredited (by the region, Ministry, or by the TF), public or private institutions that organise Master programmes, or training providers that release skills certification

[17] Indeed, elaborations of PIAAC data confirm that the low-skilled in Italy are less likely to use distance learning compared to the higher-skilled: among low-skilled adults (with PIAAC literacy scores level at 1 or below) who have participated to (job-related) learning activity (in the 12 preceding the survey), only 16% report that at least one learning activity was organised as distance learning, compared to 28% of high-skilled adults (with PIAAC literacy scores at level 4/5).

References

ANPAL (2018), "XVIII Rapporto sulla Formazione Continua", http://www.anpal.gov.it/Dati-e-pubblicazioni/Documents/XVIII-Rapporto-formazione-continua.pdf (accessed on 28 March 2018). [4]

Casano, L. et al. (2017), "Bilateralità e formazione", https://moodle.adaptland.it/mod/book/view.php?id=21892 (accessed on 7 February 2018). [21]

Eurofound (2016), "Sectoral training and development funds: the Netherlands", *Eurofound.* [8]

Eurofound (2016), "Sectoral training funds (STF): Belgium", *Eurofound.* [9]

Eurofound (2016), "Training fund in enterprises", https://www.eurofound.europa.eu/printpdf/observatories/emcc/erm/support-instrument/training-fund-in-enterprises (accessed on 3 April 2018). [13]

Fialho, P., G. Quintini and M. Vandeweyer (forthcoming), *Returns to different forms of job-related training: Factoring in informal learning*, OECD Social Employment and Migration working paper. [25]

Fondartigianato (2012), *Invito 1° - 2012 per La realizzazione di attività di formazione continua per Il sostegno e lo sviluppo dei livelli produttivi ed occupazionali Fondo Interprofessionale per la formazione continua.* [26]

Fondimpresa (2016), *Le attività di Fondimpresa*, http://www.fondimpresa.it/images/in_cifre/attivita_fondimpresa/Le_attivita_Fondimpresa_26-10-2016-sito.pdf (accessed on 28 June 2018). [12]

Fondo Formazione PMI (2017), *Finanziamento a sportello di PIani di formazione continua per lavoratori di PMI e Grandi imprese*, https://www.fondopmi.com/wp-content/uploads/2017/01/FAPI_A1-2017_SportelloImpresa_del.CDA_n.3_30032017.pdf (accessed on 12 May 2018). [20]

ILO (2017), "Upskilling SMEs", *International Labor Organization*, http://www.ilo.org/wcmsp5/groups/public/---ed_emp/---emp_ent/documents/publication/wcms_609267.pdf (accessed on 12 April 2018). [6]

Johanson, R. (2009), "A review of national training funds", *The World Bank, SP Discussion Paper No. 0922*, http://siteresources.worldbank.org/SOCIALPROTECTION/Resources/SP-Discussion-papers/Labor-Market-DP/0922.pdf (accessed on 26 June 2018). [2]

Kis, V. et al. (2008), "Learning for Jobs OECD Reviews of Vocational Education and Training Hungary", *OECD*, https://www.oecd.org/hungary/41738329.pdf (accessed on 3 April 2018). [23]

Lee, K. (2016), "Training by Small and Medium-Sized Enterprises: Innovative Cases and the Consortium Approach in the Republic of Korea", *ADBI Working Paper Series*, http://www.adb.org/publications/skills-training-small-and-medium-sized-enterprises-innovative-cases-consortium-approach-korea/ (accessed on 12 April 2018). [11]

Lee, K. and D. Sahu (2017), "Training Levy-Rebate Incentive Scheme and SME Training Consortium Program to Address Unemployment and Low Productivity in SMEs – A Korean Policy Case CASE STUDY", *Global Delivery Initiative*, http://www.globaldeliveryinitiative.org/sites/default/files/case-studies/sme_korea_case_study_final.pdf (accessed on 12 April 2018). [10]

Müller, N. and F. Behringer (2012), "Subsidies and Levies as Policy Instruments to Encourage Employer-Provided Training", *OECD Education Working Papers*, No. 80, OECD Publishing, Paris, https://dx.doi.org/10.1787/5k97b083v1vb-en. [22]

OECD (2019), *Getting Skills Right: Future-Ready Adult Learning Systems*, Getting Skills Right, OECD Publishing, Paris, https://dx.doi.org/10.1787/9789264311756-en. [16]

OECD (2017), *Educational Opportunity for all. Overcoming inequality throughout the life course*, https://www.oecd-ilibrary.org/docserver/9789264287457-en.pdf?expires=1526287982&id=id&accname=ocid84004878&checksum=60C3CF89A1F7CB65DE2C44B966DEDEA0 (accessed on 14 May 2018). [14]

OECD (2017), *Entrepreneurship at a Glance 2017*, OECD Publishing, Paris, http://dx.doi.org/10.1787/entrepreneur_aag-2017-en. [1]

OECD (2017), *Financial Incentives for Steering Education and Training*, OECD Publishing, Paris, https://dx.doi.org/10.1787/9789264272415-en. [15]

OECD (2017), *Getting Skills Right: Italy*, OECD Publishing, Paris, http://dx.doi.org/10.1787/9789264278639-en. [19]

OECD (2017), "OECD Skills Strategy Diagnostic Report: Italy", https://www.oecd.org/skills/nationalskillsstrategies/Diagnostic-report-Italy.pdf (accessed on 26 March 2018). [18]

OECD (2017), "OECD Skills Strategy Diagnostic Report: The Netherlands", https://www.oecd.org/skills/nationalskillsstrategies/OECD-Skills-Strategy-Diagnostic-Report-Netherlands.pdf (accessed on 31 March 2018). [7]

OECD (2014), *OECD Studies on SMEs and Entrepreneurship: Italy*, OECD Publishing, Paris, https://doi.org/10.1787/20780990 (accessed on 28 June 2018). [3]

OECD (forthcoming), *Training levies in Southeast Asia: what do they offer and how should they be organised? Lessons from global experience*, OECD Publishing, Paris. [24]

UNESCO (2018), *Funding skills development: The private sector contribution*, United Nations Educational, Scientific and Cultural Organization, http://unesdoc.unesco.org/images/0026/002619/261984e.pdf (accessed on 26 June 2018). [5]

Ziderman, A. (2016), “Funding Mechanisms for Financing Vocational Training: An Analytical Framework”, *IZA Policy Paper No. 110*, http://ftp.iza.org/pp110.pdf (accessed on 4 January 2018). [17]

Chapter 4. Aligning training to the skills needed in the labour market

In order for Training Funds to work effectively, not only do they need to reach many firms and workers and be inclusive, but they also need to provide training that is useful and aligned to labour market needs. Indeed, Training Funds have the potential to help firms update the skills of their employees, equip workers with the skills needed to adapt to the challenges arising from the mega-trends (technological change, ageing, globalisation), and meet the objectives of recent policy initiatives such as Industry 4.0. This Chapter analyses the mechanisms to ensure that Training Funds promote the development of skills most relevant for the labour market.

The statistical data for Israel are supplied by and under the responsibility of the relevant Israeli authorities. The use of such data by the OECD is without prejudice to the status of the Golan Heights, East Jerusalem and Israeli settlements in the West Bank under the terms of international law.

4.1. Channelling training towards skills most in shortage

Training Funds have a great potential to reduce skills imbalances – such as shortages and surpluses – in the Italian labour market. In fact, if used effectively, Training Funds can equip workers and the unemployed (see Section 6.2) with skills most needed and difficult to find by employers.

Ensuring a high level of alignment between TF-supported training and labour market needs is important from an aggregate point of view, as it could reduce overall skills imbalances, and potentially lead to enhanced firms' productivity. Moreover, good alignment to skills needs is also important for individual learners, as they can acquire the skills that bring the brightest labour market outlooks in terms of, for example, wage progression, employment, and job quality.

It is possible to analyse the extent to which TF-supported training develops the skills that are most in demand in the Italian labour market, by combining the information on skills shortages/surpluses contained in the *OECD Skills for Jobs* database (see Box 4.1), with the information on the skills developed through TF-supported training contained in the Nexus database (see Section 5.4).

More specifically, by building a crosswalk between the skills taxonomy used in the Nexus database and the *OECD Skills for Jobs* database, it is possible to compare the number of TF-supported training programmes that have been completed in each given skill (or thematic area) with the degree by which that skill is in shortage/surplus in the Italian labour market.

It is important to notice, however, that results need to be taken with caution considered the tentative nature, and limitations, of this mapping exercise (see Annex B).

Box 4.1. *OECD Skills for Jobs* database

The *OECD Skills for Jobs* database provides timely information about skills shortages – *i.e.* when skills sought by employers are not available in the pool of potential recruits – and skills surpluses – *i.e.* when the supply of certain skills is higher than the demand.

The database has key innovative features compared to existing measures of skills shortages/surpluses. By looking at skills – i.e. the set of competences mobilised to perform the tasks related to a job – rather than occupations or fields of study, the new indicators go beyond the traditional measures of imbalances. Furthermore, unlike the generally subjective information available from employer surveys, the *OECD Skills for Jobs* database draws from quantitative data derived from household surveys. Finally, the indicator is constructed using a multidimensional set of quantitative signals on skills pressure (i.e. five sub-indices, including wage growth, employment growth and unemployment), which provides a holistic interpretation of skill imbalances in the labour markets.

The skill needs indicator is constructed in two consecutive steps:

(i) in the first step, sub-indices for hourly wage growth, employment growth, unemployment rate, hours worked and under-qualification are used to provide a quantitative indication of the extent of the labour market pressure on each one of the occupations analysed. The result of this analysis returns a ranking of occupations ordered from the one most in shortage to most in surplus.

(ii) in the second step, occupations that are in shortage/surplus are mapped into the underlying skills requirements associated to those occupations, using the occupation-skills taxonomy developed by O*NET.

Information is provided at the 2-digit ISCO occupation level and is disaggregated into three domains of competence – knowledge, skills, and abilities:

- ***Knowledge*** refers to the body of information that makes adequate performance on the job possible (e.g. knowledge of plumbing for a plumber; knowledge of mathematics for an economist).
- ***Skills*** refer to the proficient manual, verbal or mental manipulation of data or things (e.g. complex problem solving; social skills)
- ***Ability*** refer to the competence to perform an observable activity (e.g. ability to plan and organise work; attentiveness; endurance).

The database covers Italy as well as most OECD countries and some emerging economies. For Italy and other selected countries, indicators are available at the regional and occupational level.

Source: OECD (2017[1]), *Getting Skills Right: Skills for Jobs Indicators*, https://doi.org/10.1787/9789264277878-en.

As shown in Figure 4.1, Training Funds seem to put efforts into developing skills that are not necessarily in high-demand in the Italian labour market. For example, while the knowledge of *computers and electronics* is in shortage in the labour market in Italy, very few TF-supported training programmes are aimed at developing ICT-related skills. While the knowledge of *computers and electronics* makes the top of the ranking of skills in demand in Italy, this is a training area that is rarely provided by Training Funds (the 4th least frequently Training Funds-provided type of training).[1] Similarly, *clerical* knowledge (the knowledge of administrative and clerical procedures such as word processing, managing files and records and other office procedures) is in strong demand in the labour market but very few TFs-supported training programmes are aimed at developing these skills: they are the top second skills need in Italy, but the least frequently Training Funds-provided type of training.[2] Conversely, many resources seem to be devoted to developing skills whose demand is mild or weak. For example, the knowledge of *manufacturing and production* is one dimension where shortages are among the lowest in the labour market. Despite that, much of the Training Funds resources are devoted to support training in this area. Indeed, this is the second lowest skills priority, yet it is the third most frequently Training Funds-provided type of training.[3]

Figure 4.1. Skills shortages and number of TF-supported training programmes, by thematic area, Italy, 2015

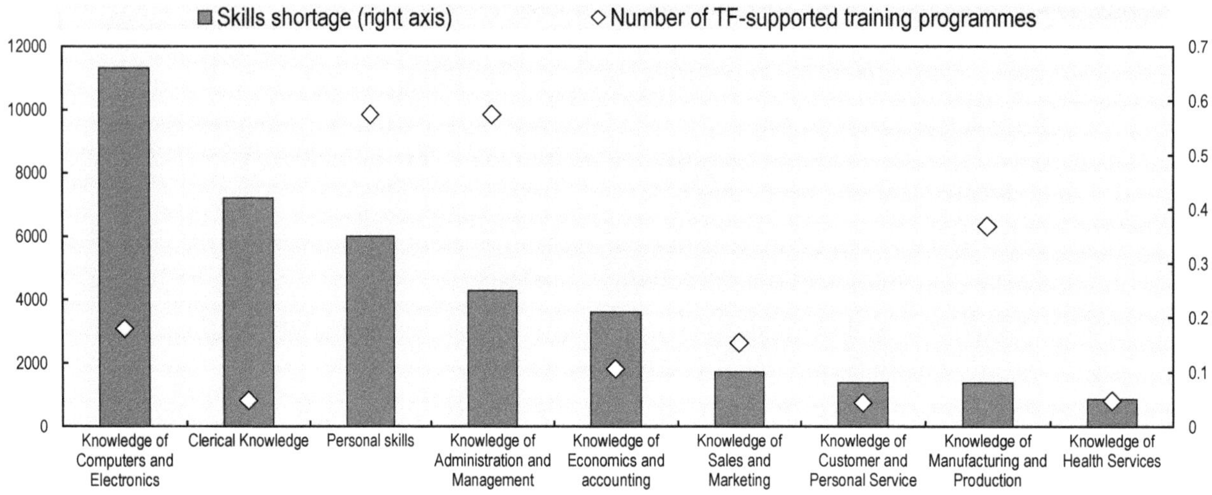

Source: Authors' elaborations based on the OECD Skills for Jobs database and the Nexus database.

Despite the above-mentioned current misalignment between skill needs and the supply of TF-supported training, the situation has been improving in recent years and things are moving in the right direction. Data for the past decade suggests that Training Funds have followed the direction of the changing dynamics of skill demands, though falling short in some cases as mentioned above.

When looking at the time evolution of skill demands and TF-supported training provision (see Figure 4.2), data show that increases in the shortage of a certain skill has been often accompanied by an increase in the number of TF-supported training aimed at filling those skill gaps. For example, knowledge of *administration and management* has been increasingly in shortage in the Italian labour market in the period 2008-2015, and the number of TF-supported training aimed at developing these skills have also increased since 2008 (although it reduced slightly in 2015). Similarly, the shortage of knowledge of *sales and marketing* has been increasing since 2008, and so as the number of TF-supported training programmes aimed at developing that skill (although it reduced in 2014-2015).

Figure 4.2. Evolution of skills shortages and TF-supported training programmes, by thematic area and year, 2008-2015

Skills shortages and number of TF-supported training programmes

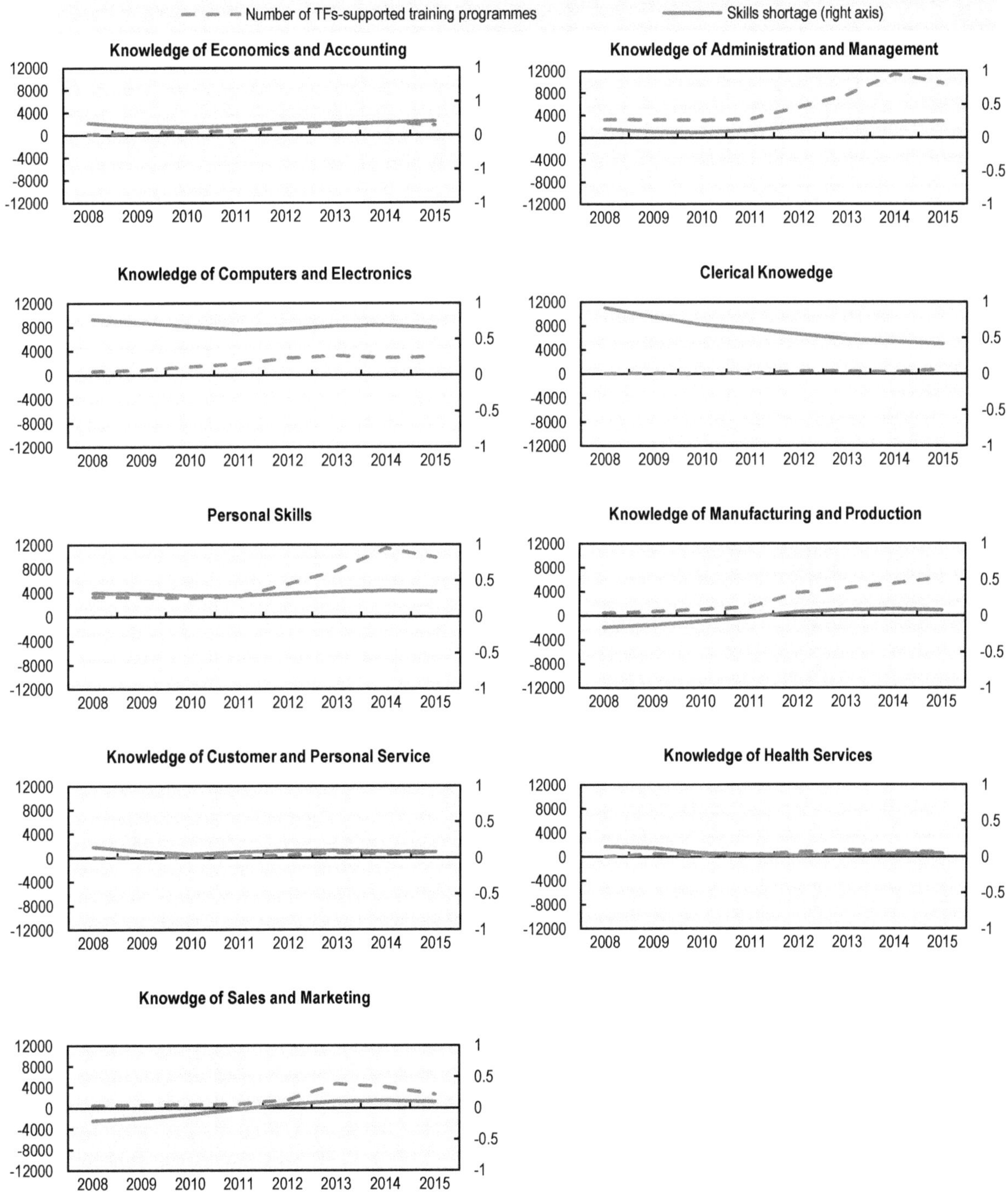

Source: Author's elaborations based on the OECD Skills for Jobs database and the Nexus database.

In terms of alignment to skills needs, Training Funds seem to perform in similar ways regardless of their size (*i.e.* the number of firms enrolled). All groups of Training Funds seem to under-invest in skills in high shortage (knowledge of *computers and electronics*; *clerical* knowledge) to a similar extent, with micro-Training Funds (covering less than 5000 firms) and large Training Funds (covering over 100 000 firms) doing slightly better (on *clerical* knowledge and knowledge of *computers and electronics*, respectively). Large and medium-sized Training Funds (*i.e.* with over 20 000 firms) seem to focus relatively more attention to training programmes that develop knowledge of *manufacturing and production* (which are not in high shortage in the labour market). On the other hand, small Training Funds (*i.e.* with between 5 000 and 20 000 firms) tend to more often focus on developing *personal skills* compared to larger and micro Training Funds (Figure 4.3).

Figure 4.3. TF-supported training, by thematic area and Training Funds size, 2015

Percentage of TF-supported training in each Training Funds group

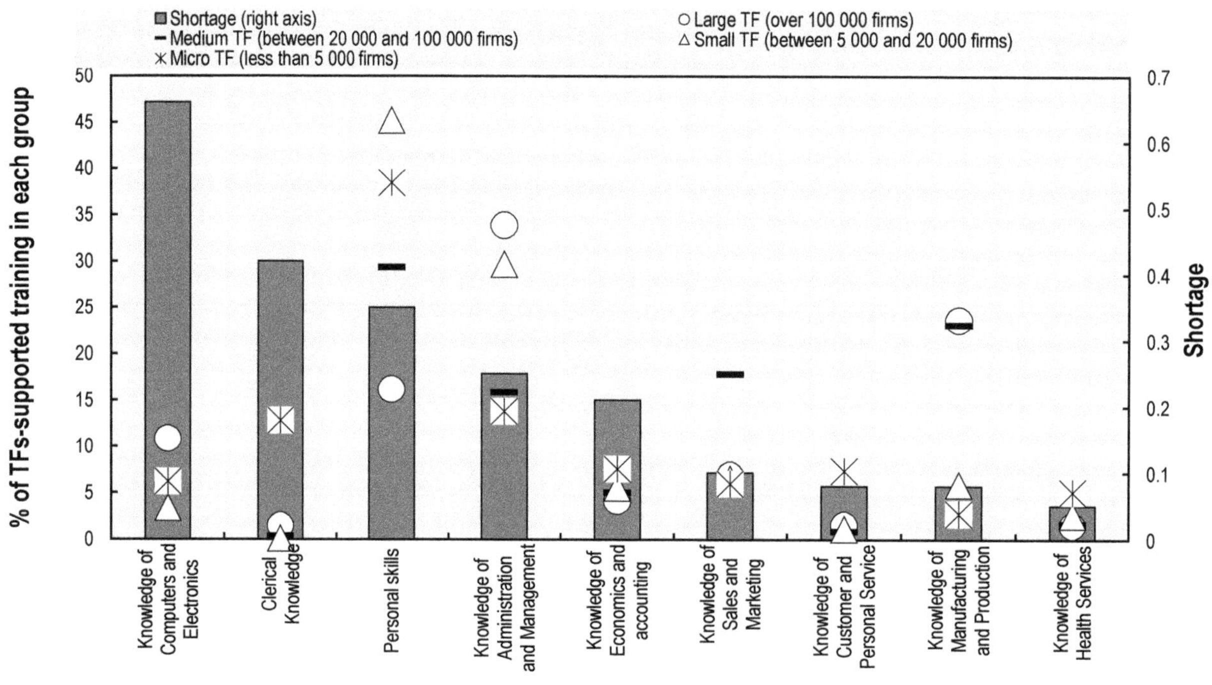

Note: Large Training Funds include Fondimpresa, Fonarcom, Fondo Artigianato Formazione, For.te; Medium Training Funds include: Formazienda, Fonditalia, Fondoprofessioni; small Training Funds include: Fon.Coop, Fondirigenti, Fond.e.r, Fondolavoro; micro Training Funds include: Fondir, Fon.ter, For.Agri, Fondo Formazione Servizi Pubblici, Fondo Banche Assicurazioni.
Source: Author's elaborations based on the OECD Skills for Jobs database and the Nexus database.

Results disaggregated at the regional level show that there is room to improve the ability of Training Funds to respond to regional/local labour market needs. Indeed, in some cases, regions seem to invest most of training programmes to develop skills that are the least demanded in the regional labour market, or even in surplus (see Figure 4.4). In Sardinia, for example, knowledge of *sales and marketing* is in surplus in the labour market, yet most TF-supported training programmes seem to be targeted on developing these skills. Similarly, in Veneto, *administration and management* knowledge, as well as *manufacturing and production* knowledge are in surplus in the labour market, yet taken together they absorb 55% of all training programmes.

Figure 4.4. Skills shortages and number of TF-supported training programmes, by thematic area and regions, Italy, 2016

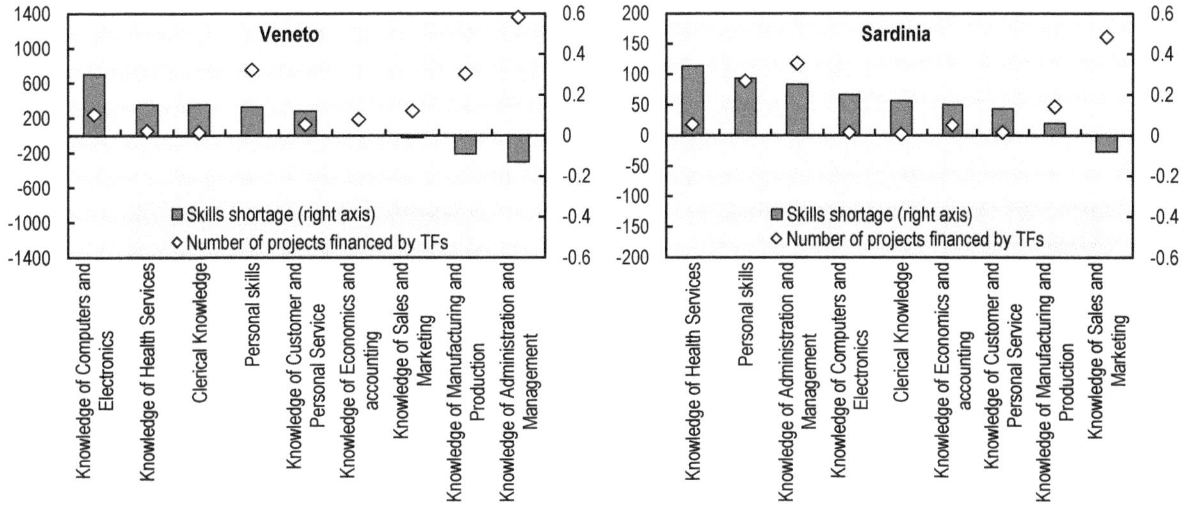

Source: Author's elaborations based on the OECD Skills for Jobs database and the Nexus database.

4.2. Strengthening the involvement of social partners

One way to ensure that training is aligned to local skills needs is to ensure that social partners' views are reflected in the various phases of training provision. Indeed, social partners are more likely to understand firms and workers' skills and training needs, and are, therefore, best placed to design appropriate training programmes that reflect the interests of workers and firms.

In theory, in Italy social partners are in a very good position to influence the various steps of the training offer financed by the Training Funds. Indeed, by law the management board of Training Funds must be composed by representatives of social partners – in equal number from trade unions and employers' organisations (see Section 2.2). This should ensure that funding allocation reflects the priorities agreed through social partners' representation.

Moreover, by law all training proposals must be agreed between social partner representatives, and no plan can be submitted for funding without approval from trade unions' representatives. This is similar to what happens in other OECD countries – *e.g.* in Spain – where firms' applications to the levy scheme need to be reviewed by the firm's worker representatives before being approved (OECD, 2017[2]).

In a view to ensure that trade unions involvement is close to learners' needs, trade unions' approval must take place at the level closest to the beneficiary, i.e. at the firm or territorial level (depending on the type of training plan) or at national level as a last resort option. To further strengthen concertation practices, recently ANPAL guidelines have established that the agreement has to take place between social partners outside of Training Funds management boards.

On top of the above-mentioned legal framework, some Training Funds have also been taking steps to strengthen concertation practices and ensure that both employers' organisations and trade unions have a say in defining the TF skills agenda. For instance, in *Fondimpresa*, employers' organisations (*i.e.* Confindustria) and trade unions (*i.e.*

CGIL, CISL, UIL) meet at least once a year in a strategic Committee (*Comitato di Indirizzo Strategico*) with the aim to jointly identify the key skills priorities and determine how to best use the resources of the *collective account*.

While in theory these rules should pave the way for effective collaboration among social partners, and despite the fact that some Training Funds have been taking steps to strengthen concertation procedures, in practice various observers notice how social dialogue around TF-supported training remains weak and could be improved. Oftentimes, – especially in the context of *individual accounts* – training plans are developed by firms, employers' organisations, or training providers, while approval by trade unions is only formal (Casano et al., 2017[3]).

An online survey conducted among firms[4] registered in *Fondirigenti* shows that the role of social partners in the various stages of the TF-supported training offer – from the definition of training needs, through the development of the training plan, to the financing and delivery of training programmes – is virtually inexistent, and much less important than the role played by other actors (*e.g.* training providers, consulting firms) (Fondirigenti, n.d.[4]). It has to be noted, however, that in Training Funds for employed managers (such as *Fondirigenti*, but also *Fondir* and *Fondo Dirigenti PMI*) social dialogue is weaker than in the other Training Funds, considered that managers often negotiates their training directly with firms. If a similar survey was carried out in other Training Funds, it would probably show less pessimistic results.

There are many reasons behind this lack of social dialogue between employers' organisations and trade unions around TF-supported training. One relates to the fragmentation of the Italian social partners system.

Italy counts a plethora of employers' organisations and trade unions compared to what can typically be observed in the OECD area. Indeed, Italy has the 2nd highest number of employers' organisations (after Israel) and trade unions (after Turkey) in the OECD area (see Figure 4.5). This fragmentation is also reflected in the composition of Training Funds, as some of them count as many as 8 different employers' organisations or trade unions. Within this fragmented context, coming to an agreement on training priorities can be challenging, especially when social partners within the same TF cover different sectors/industries.[5]

Figure 4.5. Number of employer and union confederations, Italy and OECD countries

Number of active confederations, 2015 or latest available year

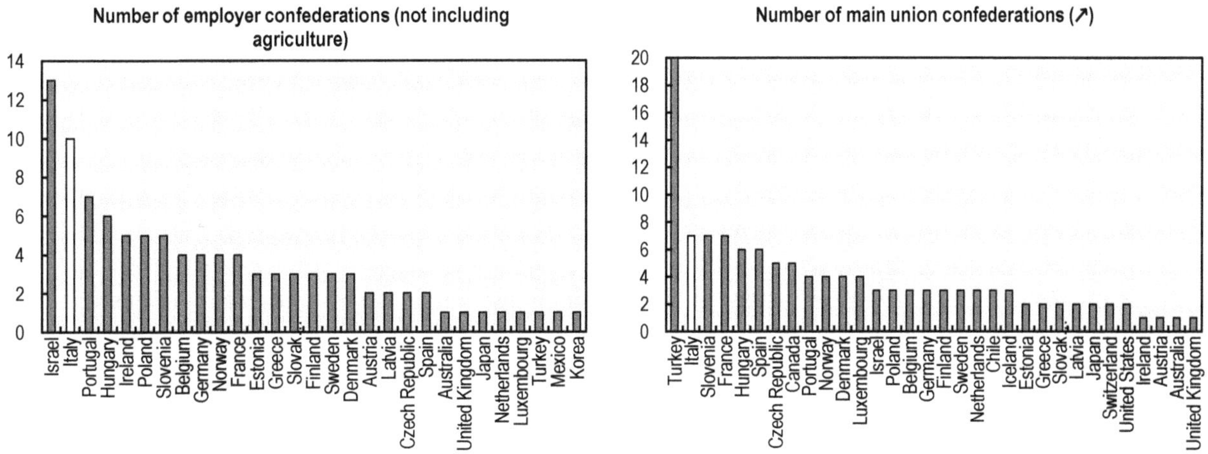

Source: J. Visser, ICTWSS Data base. version 5.1. Amsterdam: Amsterdam Institute for Advanced Labour Studies (AIAS), University of Amsterdam, September 2016 and OECD Policy Questionnaire.

It is also possible that, in a view to simplify administrative procedures for firms (especially SMEs – see Chapter 2), Training Funds have found ways to make the involvement of social partners much less binding and stringent – effectively weakening their role and engagement. To give one example, several Training Funds consider "tacit consent" as a sufficient proof of approval by trade unions. While some Training Funds penalise the use of tacit consent – *Foncoop*, for instance, gives a lower score to, and sometimes even forbids the financing of, training plans that have been approved through this simplified procedure – in most cases this practice is widely tolerated.

Moreover, according to many stakeholders, the use of *individual accounts* – especially by larger firms (see Section 2.2) – tends to weaken the role of social partners by reducing Training Funds to a mere "cash dispenser" (Casano et al., 2017[3]). Some Training Funds have decided to forbid the use of this financing channel specifically to give social partners (rather than individual firms) more voice in Training Funds training decisions (e.g. *Fondo Banche e Assicurazioni*)[6].

But much of the challenge of weak social dialogue around continuous learning relates to the inability of trade unions to appropriately identify and represent workers' training needs. Because Training Funds' budgets are financed through employer-based contributions, trade unions' representatives often struggle to make their voice heard by firms and sometimes feel that their views are not adequately taken into account in firms' training decisions.

Another possible explanation, often quoted by stakeholders, behind the weak role played by trade unions in shaping social dialogue around TF-supported training is the pressure on union members from the other (non-learning related) issues in members' working lives such as redundancies, pay freezes, employment contracts, which have grown importance especially in the context of the economic crisis.[7]

Lack of involvement by trade unions in TF-supported training decisions may also reflect the lack of trade unionists' ability to understand workers' skills needs. Some stakeholders, in fact, argue that trade unionists are often far from the productive structure of firms, they lack a deep understanding of firms' development strategies, and as such they are ill-prepared to understand the training needs of the workers they represent.

Isolated good practice examples – to ensure that trade unions understand well the skills needs of workers – do exist, however. The national collective agreement of the chemistry industry appointed a "training delegate" (*delegato alla formazione*), a trade union representative whose main role is to develop a deep understanding of the workers' skills needs within the sector, and help shape training plans accordingly. This is a very good practice example that could be extended to trade unionists in other industries/sectors.

Going forward, trade unions need to continue engaging much more in the development of the skills of the workforce. Perhaps Italy could learn from the experience of OECD countries that have taken steps to better involve social partners in adult learning, which span from efforts to train trade unionists; include skills issues into the collective bargaining agenda; develop networks on adult learning; and create dedicated positions for trade union specialists on training (see Box 4.2) (OECD, 2019[5]).

Box 4.2. Involve social partners in adult learning: the experience of OECD countries

In **Belgium**, training of workers' representatives at the company level is an important element of adult learning. Several branches have specific agreements between the social partners, whereby employers pay for the training of workers' representatives and allow their participation to training during working hours.

In **Germany**, the discussion of training opportunities is part of works council rights and duties, as specified in the Works Council Constitution Act (TUAC, 2016[36]). Skills issues are consistently included in the bargaining agenda. For example in the 2014 bargaining round many national agreements included issues such as the continued employment of apprentices after the completion of their training, incentives for lifelong learning, and periods of paid educational leave.

In **Switzerland** since 2017, *Movendo*, the institute for the training of trade unions (*Institut de formation des syndicats*) has developed a network of ambassadors for continuous learning.

In the **United Kingdom**, over the past 10 years there has been a major change in union engagement with skills. The great majority of unions now include Union Learning Representatives (ULRs) in their management structures. Many unions have established learning committees at regional and/or national level. For example, 25% of all the motions and amendments to the 2014 TUC annual Congress were related in some way to education. There are around 450 jobs within Unions that relate to supporting skills, around 15-20% of all union employment (TUAC, 2016[6]).

4.3. Making use of existing skills assessment and anticipation (SAA) exercises to establish training priorities

Skills assessment and anticipation (SAA) exercises – *i.e.* tools used to generate information on current and future skills needs – are fundamental to understand what are the skills most demanded in the labour market (OECD, 2016[7]).

In Italy, there is a plethora of SAA exercises. They are developed by different institutions, produce various types of skill needs information, provide data at different levels of aggregation, and cover a number of time spans (current, short- and medium-term forecasts) (OECD, 2017[8]).

SAA information can represent a very useful tool for Training Funds. It can orient Training Funds' training strategies, and help Training Funds prioritise and channel resources towards the programmes that develop the skills most demanded in the labour market.

For example, some Training Funds develop thematic public calls (*avvisi*) drawing from the results of SAA exercises. In some Training Funds (*e.g.* Fondir), there is a dedicated committee – whose components are nominated by social partners – that uses existing SAA information to develop public calls in line with skills demanded in the labour market. Other Training Funds (e.g. *Fondimpresa*) have developed a research centre that – among other activities – uses available SAA information to select training priorities and develop public calls accordingly.

Oftentimes, however, in the views of many Training Funds, available SAA information to Training Funds is not fit for purpose. Sometimes the information collected is not sufficiently up-to-date to measure the pulse of the labour market in real time. Sometimes, data sources are not sufficiently disaggregated at the regional level, and/or do not use nomenclatures (*e.g.* on skills and competences) comparable to what the Training Funds typically use. Another key challenge is that SAA information is often scattered across different sources, potentially making use and interpretation by Training Funds difficult (OECD, 2017[8]).

When SAA information is lacking in certain sectors, occupations, regions, or is not detailed or specific enough, some Training Funds have been taking steps to carry out their own SAA exercises. To give one example, the largest TF for (employed) managers (*Fondirigenti*) conducts foresight exercises through a series of focus groups engaging over 400 different stakeholders throughout the territory. The focus groups have the intent to open a dialogue with member partners – including enterprises, social partners, and training providers that work with *Fondirigenti* – to understand emerging training needs among managers.

4.4. Assisting firms and workers to better understand their skills and training needs

In order to make good training decisions, firms and workers need to be aware of their skill needs, the value of training and up-skilling, and the training opportunities available. Oftentimes, however, Italian firms – especially SMEs – and workers are not aware of their skill and training needs. As a result, TF-supported training is still too often supply-oriented, *i.e.* it reflects what training providers are able to offer, rather than what firms and workers actually need (Valsega, 2017[9]).[8]

Training Funds can play a great role in assisting firms and workers to identify their skill and training needs, and many are already taking steps in this direction. For example, some Training Funds are:

- **Financing firms to conduct SAA exercises**: for example, "Grant n.40" promoted by *Foncoop* is structured in two phases: in the first phase, firms are financed to carry out an SAA exercise among their employees; in the second phase, *Foncoop* finances the training course based on the skill needs emerged in the SAA exercise.

Similarly, "Grant n.35" requires that at least 30% of funding is devoted to activities other than training, such as skills assessment within the firms. This approach is systematically adopted in some OECD countries. For example, in Poland, employers can use National Training Fund resources to finance the diagnosis of training needs (UNESCO, 2016[10]).

- **Assigning a higher score to training plans that draw on high-quality SAA information**. This practice is currently undertaken by some Training Funds (*e.g.* Fondimpresa, Fondoprofessioni). The specificity, relevance, methodology of the SAA exercises, as well as the alignment of the objectives of the proposed training plan to SAA results, are factors that are evaluated in the selection process and which contribute to the determination of the training plan's final score and thus its likelihood of being financed.
- **Providing career guidance to workers**. *Fondirigenti,* for instance, has developed an on-line skills assessment tool for managers, which, after completion, returns a snapshot of the strengths and weaknesses of the respondent compared to benchmark workers in other Italian firms. This information can then be used to identify training programmes that are tailored to the respondent's needs. Similarly, *Forma.temp* has developed an app where individuals can take a test to better understand the skills they need. These on-line tools or apps, if extended and used by all Training Funds, may be particularly useful for SMEs where it is particularly challenging to carry out skills analysis at the firm level.

Despite these many innovative and interesting examples – however – Training Funds efforts to help firms/workers to assess their skill and training needs tend to remain quite limited and could be expanded. Indeed, the vast majority (93.7%) of all training programmes financed by the Training Funds are not integrated by any career guidance or skills assessment activity (see Table 4.1) (ANPAL, 2018[11]). Assistance/support activities are not systematic and structured enough and remain only at the margins of Training Funds' core activities, probably reflecting the fact that there is no obligation for Training Funds to assist firms in the analysis of their skills needs, nor are Training Funds required to link funding to firms' skills assessment/anticipation analysis.

Table 4.1. Types of TF-supported training programmes (approved), 2016

	Number of training programmes	% of training programmes
Standard (only training)	160 667	93.7
Integrated with skills assessment activities	5 976	3.5
Integrated with guidance activities	1 174	0.7
Integrated with guidance support for mobility/outplacement/relocation	380	0.2
Integrated with support services for certain types of beneficiaries	22	0.0
Data not declared	3 171	1.9
Total	170 656	100.0

1. Data refers to January 2016 to December 2016. Data includes programmes approved in 2015 and started in 2016.
2. The question provides multiple answer choices. Therefore the sum of the answers is higher than the total of programmes approved. For the calculation of "% of training programmes" the sum of the individual answers is used.

Source: ANPAL's elaborations based on the Nexus Database.

Perhaps Italy could benefit from the experience of OECD countries that have a training levy in place and have taken steps to help firms (especially SMEs) to articulate their skill needs. In Belgium, Sectoral Training Funds provide firms with advice and support around issues such as developing training plans or corporate training policies (Eurofound, 2016[14]). In the Netherlands, some of the sectoral funds have advisors visiting and supporting small firms to identify and formulate their training needs (OECD, 2017[2]). Other sectoral funds have developed online platforms to provide targeted support. For example, OTIB – the sectoral training fund related to building services engineering – supports SMEs by offering a platform with online HR-tools: the OTIB-skillsmanager. The platform provides SMEs with a framework for defining job profiles, scanning employees' skills in relation to job requirements, and addressing skills development in line with the organisation's need for innovation (OECD, 2017[7]).

4.5. Reacting quickly to firms' changing skill needs

In the context of rapidly changing labour markets, one key prerequisite to ensure that training is aligned to firms' skill needs is to make sure that Training Funds react quickly to the needs expressed by firms and workers. Lengthy administrative procedures to access funding, for example, may lead to a deferral of enterprise training and persistent skill gaps during the waiting period.

Training Funds have already taken various steps to ensure that they are able to finance training as rapidly as possible. Indeed, administrative procedures and paperwork to access funds are already kept to a minimum by virtually all Training Funds (see Chapter 2). Moreover – both of the financing channels made available by Training Funds (individual and collective accounts) can be accessed quite rapidly by firms.[9]

Despite these positive steps, however, there are challenges that could hamper the ability of Training Funds to respond quickly to firms and workers' changing skill needs. Similarly to levy-grant schemes in other countries, Training Funds involve many case-by-case decisions and management competences, which can be demanding and time-consuming in administrative terms (UNESCO, 2018[12]). [10] Moreover, the Law on State Aids has burdened Training Funds with onerous administrative procedures which have likely made them less agile and responsive to changing firms' skill needs (see Chapter 1).

4.6. Equipping workers with ICT skills needed for the digital transformation

The Italian workforce seems to be ill-equipped with ICT skills. A survey conducted by ISTAT shows that 71.7% of the Italian population reports having no (3.3%), low (33.3%) or only basic (35.1%) ICT skills (ISTAT, 2016[13]).

In the international context, Italy is lagging behind. According to the Survey of Adult Skills (PIAAC), almost 40% of Italian adults (aged 15-65) lack computer skills, the second highest share across the OECD only preceded by Poland (see Figure 4.6) (OECD, 2017[14]; OECD, 2013[15]).

These results are corroborated by the Europe's Digital Progress Report (EDPR) – which tracks the progress made by Member States in terms of their digitisation and shows how in the Human Capital dimension Italy is performing well below the average and is making little progress (European Commission, 2017[16]).

While equipping adults with adequate ICT skills could potentially contribute to economic progress, firms' innovativeness, and productivity, it could also translate into better career options for workers with these skills. A recent study conducted in the Lombardy region shows that, within the same occupations, workers with digital (and in particular, Industry 4.0) skills benefit from a wage premium of 2%; a premium that increases to 16% when age-related wage progression is accounted for (Fioni, 2018[17]).

Figure 4.6. Computer skills among adults, Italy and OECD countries

Percentage share of adults (15-65) with no ICT experience

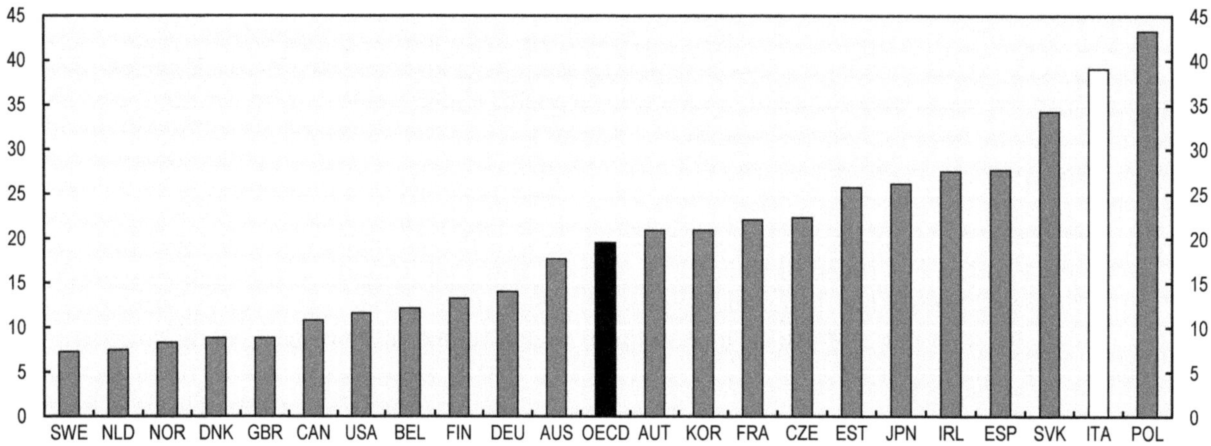

Source: OECD Skills Outlook 2013 Database.

In this context, Training Funds have a great role to play to ensure that workers are equipped with the skills needed for the digital transformation. Some Training Funds have already started investing resources in this direction. To give just few illustrative examples among many:

- *Fondimpresa*, since 2011, has established a dedicated budget line to technological innovation, and regularly promotes thematic grants (the so-called "*Avvisi Competitività*") that exclusively finance training programmes related to technological innovation, digitalisation, e-commerce, and so forth. Since 2007, *Fondimpresa* has spent EUR 346 million for competitiveness and innovation alone (Fondimpresa, 2017[18]).
- Even smaller Training Funds are taking steps in this direction. For example, *Fondo Formazione PMI* (FAPI) proposes training focussed on cybersecurity and cybercrime (ANPAL, 2018[11]).
- Some TF (e.g. *Fondo Banche e Assicurazioni*) give a higher score to training plans which include an Industry 4.0 component/dimension, thereby increasing the likelihood of these training plans to receive funding.

Despite these positive initiatives, going forward more systematic efforts by all Training Funds will be needed. While overall Training Funds' investments in ICT skills – as measured by the number of projects, the number of training hours, and the financial resources (in EUR) destined to this thematic area – have increased over the past decade in absolute terms (reflecting overall expansion of the activities of Training Funds), they have decreased compared to other thematic areas.

Indeed, while in 2008 the number of TF-supported training programmes aimed at developing ICT skills represented 6.3% of all programmes, this share has decreased to 3.2% in 2016; the number of training hours devoted to ICT skills also decreased from 7.4% to 4.3% in the same period, similarly to the share of EUR devoted to ICT skills which fell from 7% to 3.6% (see Table 4.2).

Table 4.2. Training Funds' investments into ICT skills, 2008-2016

Number of projects, number of training hours, and EUR invested in ICT skills

	Number of projects concluded	% of total number of projects	Number of training hours	% of total n. of training hours	EUR	% of total EUR
2008	664	6.3%	20 253.00	7.4%	7 421 642.07	7.0%
2009	841	5.8%	34 771.20	6.9%	29 992 987.34	11.6%
2010	1 396	8.3%	47 689.50	7.9%	16 833 799.10	6.4%
2011	1 849	9.4%	59 236.50	7.9%	19 936 025.43	7.0%
2012	2 841	6.6%	89 577.75	6.1%	19 237 657.37	5.4%
2013	3 262	4.7%	113 898.08	5.6%	28 353 459.58	5.1%
2014	2 901	3.8%	94 851.25	4.3%	18 436 885.21	4.2%
2015	3 080	4.1%	93 972.00	4.3%	17 729 754.00	4.1%
2016	1 451	3.2%	65 576.50	4.3%	9 252 832.57	3.6%

Note: Data refer to the thematic area "*informatica*". See Annex B.
Source: ANPAL's elaborations based on the Nexus database.

Decreasing Training Funds investments in ICT skills – relative to other skills areas – may partly reflect a weak demand by firms. Indeed, several Training Funds observe how take up by firms on this particular thematic area remains low. Indeed, anecdotal evidence gathered through stakeholders' interviews show that thematic grants devoted to ICT (or Industry 4.0) skills often remain underused with considerable unspent surpluses being accrued by the Training Funds. This is in stark contrast with what can generally be observed for training aimed at developing other types of skills – for which funding is often exhausted well-before the deadline, requiring subsequent re-funding (ANPAL, 2018[11]).

The low demand for "Industry 4.0" skills partly reflects the productive structure of the Italian economy, characterised by many small, often family-led, businesses, which are often concentrated in traditional sectors (see Chapter 2).[11]

In this context, it is unlikely that greater efforts on the supply-side by the Training Funds – alone – will be sufficient to raise "Industry 4.0" skills. Accompanying actions on the demand side, through effective industrial policy, will be essential.

The previous government took important steps in this direction. In 2016, the Ministry of Economic Development (hereafter MISE) developed an "Industry 4.0" plan which included a set of ambitious industrial policies aimed at shifting the Italian productive system towards the use of new and high value-added technologies (OECD, 2017[19]).[12] [13]

In a view to complement the Industry 4.0 plan and equip workers with the competences needed for the digital transformation, the 2018 Budget Law introduces – on a pilot basis and for the period of one year – the Tax Credit 4.0 (*Credito di Imposta Formazione 4.0*). The Tax Credit is designed to cover 40% of labour costs, for the entire duration of the training, for a maximum of EUR 300 thousand per firm per year. In order to be able to benefit from the measure, firms need to provide training on "Industry 4.0 skills" – including ICT and production techniques (MISE & MEF, 2017[20]).

While the Tax Credit 4.0 came with some delay with respect to the initial Industry 4.0 plan, it has great potential to increase the demand for "Industry 4.0" skills by firms and potentially encourage firms to make better use of Training Funds. Indeed, the way the Tax Credit 4.0 is designed – the fact that it focusses on reimbursing the sunk costs associated with training (time), rather than the cost of the training itself – makes the instrument not only compatible, but also complementary, to the activities of the Training Funds.

4.7. Shifting the focus away from compulsory training, such as occupational health and safety

Some training courses are compulsory for all Italian workers, for example training on occupational health and safety (OHS)[14]. Other training courses are mandatory for certain categories of workers. For instance, professionals enrolled in a professional register (e.g. engineers, architects, lawyers) are obliged to participate in training aimed at an ongoing updating of their professional skills [15] (Socci and Principi, 2014[21]).

One of the most controversial aspects of the Training Funds is the significant use of resources to financing compulsory training, particularly OHS. Indeed, despite improvements in recent years,[16] this remains by far the most common type of training programmes financed by the Training Funds, representing over 30% of all training programmes concluded. Wide differences exist across regions, with OHS representing less than 15% of all training programmes in some regions (*i.e.* Lazio) and reaching over 40% in others (*e.g.* Friuli Venezia Giulia; Sardinia) (see Figure 4.7).

Figure 4.7. TF-supported training in Occupational Health and Safety, 2016

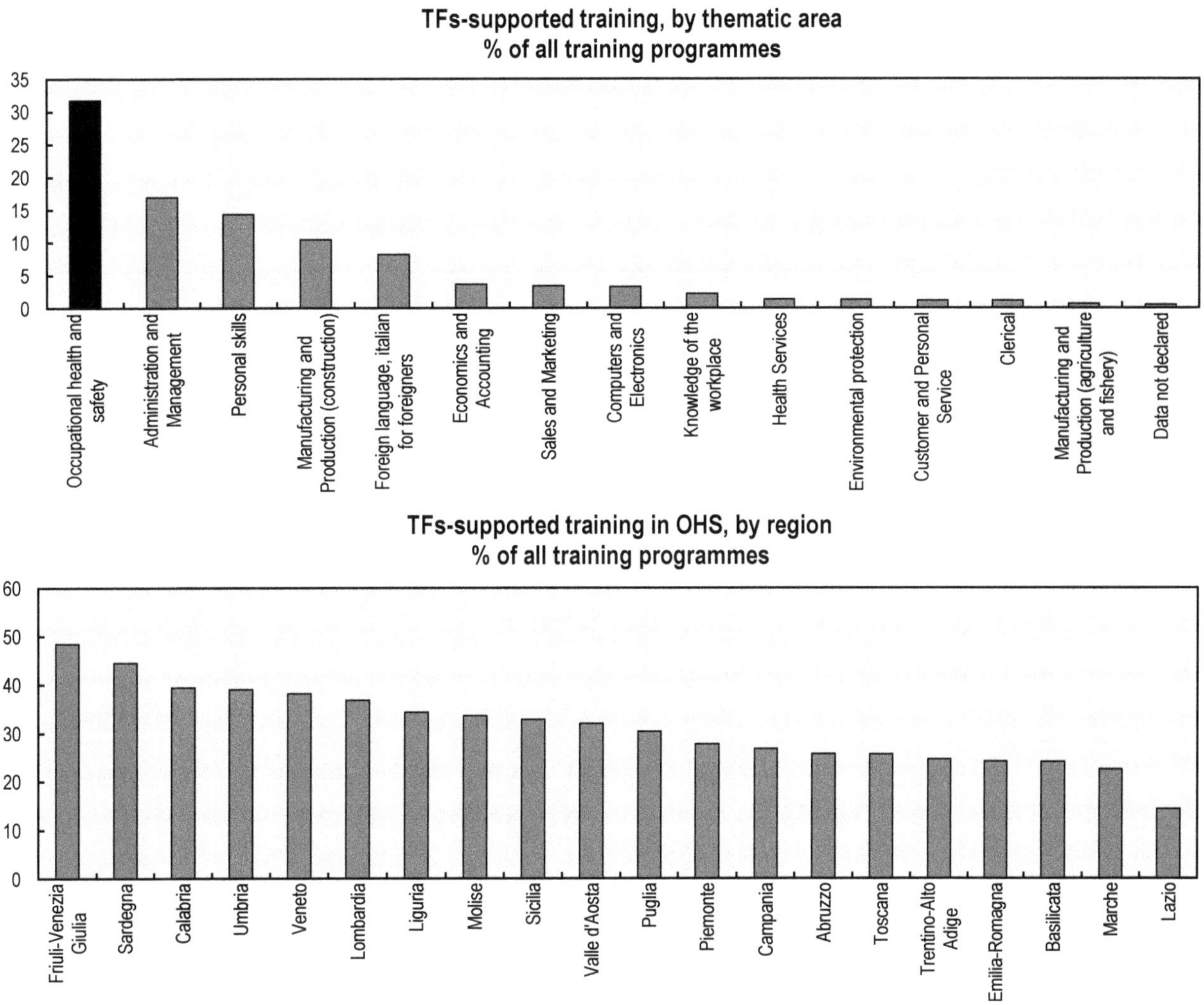

Note:

1. The question provides multiple answer choices. Therefore the sum of the answers is higher than the total of programmes approved. For the calculation of % the sum of the individual answers is used.
2. Data refers to training plans concluded.
3. Data refers to the period January 2016-December 2016.
4. For the nomenclatures originally used in the Nexus database (in Italian), see Annex A.

Source: ANPAL's elaborations of the Nexus database.

Overall, investments in compulsory training are higher in Italy compared to other countries. Indeed, in Italy compulsory training accounts for 32.8% of all training hours among firms (with at least 10 employees), the second highest share across European OECD countries after the Czech Republic (39.3%), well above the average of 20.6% and much greater than Denmark where it accounts for less than 10% of all training (Figure 4.8).[17]

Figure 4.8. Compulsory training, Italy and OECD countries, 2015

% of training hours on compulsory training

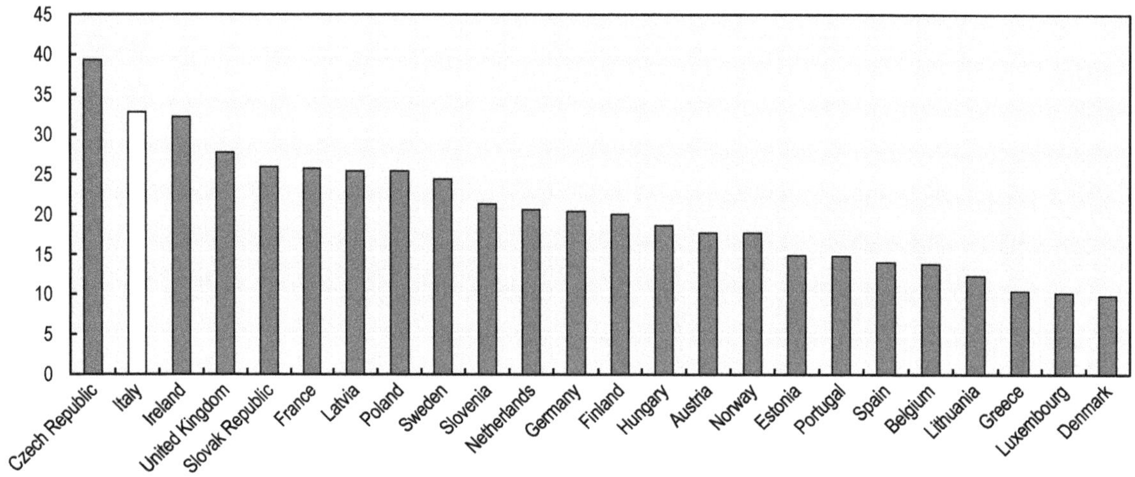

Source: CVTS 2015.

According to several stakeholders, there are at least four reasons as to why Training Funds often channel resources to this type of training. (i) Firms – especially SMEs – are often unaware of their training needs (see section 4.4) and are unprepared to conceive training proposals to apply for Training Funds funding, which may push them to finance the training that is most easily and readily available to them, including OHS. (ii) Given the high cost of labour in Italy, firms – especially SMEs – may use TF to recover at least some of these costs.[18] (iii) In the context of the crisis, the private resources available to firms to finance obligatory training (including OHS) have reduced, pushing firms to use TF funding to comply to training obligations (Casano et al., 2017[3]). (iv) The limited amount of time firms have to use funding through their individual account (two years) before resources feed back into collective accounts may give little time to firms to prepare well-developed and innovative training plans, and may push firms to quickly use available resources to finance OHS training courses instead.[19]

On the one hand, allowing firms to use Training Funds for compulsory training can have positive spillover effects, as it can bring firms closer to training programmes more generally. Indeed, for many firms – especially SMEs – it is the need to meet training obligations that pushes them to enrol in a TF in the first place. Once enrolled in a TF, these firms end up using funding not only for compulsory training but also to help their workers develop skills that are useful (e.g. ICT).

On the other hand, however, using Training Funds to finance training that is compulsory is questionable for several reasons. First of all, it risks generating large deadweight losses, *i.e.* financing training that would have taken place even in the absence of the subsidy, and therefore may represent a waste of resources. While some element of deadweight is inevitable, efforts should be taken to minimise its scale, so that the funding coming from the training levy can substantially add to the volume and quality of training.

Moreover, in a context where Italian workers lack ICT skills (see section 4.6) and have low proficiency in literacy and numeracy (see Chapter 1), the allocation of a large share of Training Funds resources to training on OHS frustrates the original objectives of the

Training Funds, which relate to providing workers with the skills needed to adapt to the future challenges in the labour market (OECD, 2017[8]; Valsega, 2017[9]).

Last but not least, extensive use of funding for OHS training can generate an unhealthy competitive environment by creating perverse incentives for TF to attract firms – especially SMEs – that are not interested in other types of training (Casano et al., 2017[3]). Indeed, some of the "newest" TF attempt to attract SMEs by giving them flexibility on how to use funding – e.g. establishing "aggregated" enterprise accounts – so that they can easily use resources to carry training on OHS (see Section 5.3).

Some steps in the right direction have already been undertaken. The Law on State Aids – which today applies to the resources directly managed by the Training Funds (*i.e.* the collective accounts) (see Section 2.3.2) – limits the use of funds for compulsory training, including OHS.[20]

Legislation aside, some of the Training Funds have also taken good steps to channel resources for financing training other than OHS. *Fondoprofessioni*, for instance, has made an agreement with the National Bilateral Body for Professional Firms (*Ente Bilaterale Nazionale per gli Studi Professionali*, E.BI.PRO.). According to the agreement, (i) E.BI.PRO reimburses 60% of the costs associated with training on OHS to its partner firms, under the condition that training is delivered by training providers accredited by *Fondoprofessioni* (E.Bi.Pro, 2017[22]); and (ii) a higher reimbursement rate (80% of the cost) is allowed if the firm is registered in *Fondoprofessioni*.

Going forward, it could be envisaged to forbid the use of Training Funds for training on OHS altogether. This would reduce deadweight losses, favour the development of a healthier competitive environment across all Training Funds, and potentially steer resources towards the development of more relevant skills.

This prohibition, however, would need to be accompanied with complementary policies aimed at strengthening the monitoring system to ensure that firms continue providing compulsory training even in the absence of TF funding.

There is also a need to change the mentality of firms to ensure that OHS is perceived as civic obligation for the firm and a right for the worker, rather than an obligation that firms need to comply to and that subtracts time and resources to firms' activities (Casano et al., 2017[3]).

Finally, Italy could envisage to increase the time available to firms to use the resources available in their individual accounts, before resources feed back into collective accounts. This would allow firms to have sufficient time to conceive training programmes that are suited to the need of the company, with an aim to steer resources away from OHS and towards achieving firms' innovation and productivity.

Notes

[1] Data are limited to those skills analysed in the chart (see Annex B). For the full skills in shortage /surpluses in Italy, see the OECD skills for jobs database.

[2] Ibidem.

[3] Ibidem.

[4] The research was conducted among "active" firms, *i.e.* firms that have adhered to at least one training plan financed by *Fondirigenti*. In total, 655 firms responded to the survey, representing 14% of all potential respondents. Results need to be taken with caution due to the possibility of a selection bias effect.

[5] It was anecdotally communicated to the OECD that communication among social partners is typically smoother among Training Funds composed by only 1 trade union and 1 employers' organisation. These include: Fonarcom; Fondirigenti; Fondo Dirigenti PMI; Formazienda; Fonditalia; Fondo Lavoro; Fondo Conoscenza.

[6] Despite covering mainly very large firms, *Fondo Banche e Assicurazioni* does not use this financing channel (typically used by larger firms). On average, this TF counts firms with over 300 employees, compared to an average of 10.6 employees among all Training Funds (ANPAL, 2018[11])

[7] Indeed, over the past years, trade unionists have focused their attention to the unemployed, their income protection, and redundancy packages, while far less attention was put into workers' training and re-skilling. Moreover, according to some stakeholders, the lack of attention paid by trade unions to training issues also reflects workers' own priorities and attitudes towards training. Italian workers' main concerns have lately been focussed on securing a stable job, receiving decent wages, and benefiting from well-protected employment contracts – priorities which have likely contributed to shaping trade unions' priority agenda.

[8] This is partly due to the fact that in most cases training providers are allowed to submit training programmes to Training Funds for funding (via collective accounts).

[9] The *individual accounts* by definition provide firms with direct and quick access to funding, and some Training Funds apply "first-come-first-served" procedures (*avvisi a sportello*) to finance training plans through the *collective account*, which provides firms with a faster access to funding compared to other grant procedures (see Section 5.2.2).

[10] This is true especially compared to other types of levy schemes available in other countries (*e.g.* France).

[11] Indeed, in Italy, the vast majority of enterprises (95%) are micro-businesses, *i.e.* enterprises with fewer than ten persons employed - a high share compared to OECD countries like Canada, New Zealand, Switzerland, and the United States, and where only 80% of less of firms are micro-businesses (see OECD SDBS database).

[12] These measures include, among others, incentives to acquire new technological equipment. For instance, a "hyper and super-depreciation" tax benefit scheme has been designed for firms investing in new tangible assets, devices and technologies enabling companies' transformation to "Industry 4.0" standards (OECD, 2017[19]).

[13] The reforms are already showing results. For example, over 60% of manufacturing firms that benefit from super-depreciation schemes find the measure useful to promote new investments (MISE & MEF, 2017[20]). The Industry 4.0 plan also managed to raise awareness about 4.0

technologies. While in 2016, 38% of firms did not know about "Industry 4.0", the figure has drastically dropped to 8% in 2017 (Osservatorio, 2017[24]).

14 In 2012, the State/Regions Agreement has made training for workers in the field of health and safety at the workplace mandatory, in a view to fulfil training obligations of employees in this field (Legislative Decree 81/2008).

15 This mandatory training of professionals is regulated by the Professions Reform Act (Decree of the President of the Republic 137/2012). Law 81/2017 establishes that 100% of the costs of mandatory continuous training (including travel expenses) of professionals enrolled in a professional register, or the self-employed, are deductible for a maximum of EUR 10 000 per year.

16 Since 2014 the share of programmes financed (and workers involved) in OHS has halved (ANPAL, 2018[11]).

17 Using training levies to fund mandatory training is a challenge that Italy shares with other countries. In Spain, for example, the State Foundation for Professional Training (*Fundación Estatal para la Formación en el Empleo*) places no restrictions on the type of training that can be covered by levy funds. As a result, most firms use them to pay for mandatory workplace training, like OHS, rather than addressing skill needs (OECD, 2017[25]). Similarly, in the United Kingdom, the vast majority of participants of the Small Firm Development Accounts scheme used the programme to provide training that they had already planned on carrying out, and would have done even if the scheme had not been in place (UNESCO, 2018[12]; Müller and Behringer, 2012[23]).

18 Employers' social security contributions (SSCs) represent 24.17% of total labour costs – the highest share in the OECD only after France (26.77%), and around 10 percentage points above the OECD average of 14.38%. Data refer to a single person without children, earning the average wage.

19 The fact that the government – in the past years – has withdrawn resources from the TF – *e.g.* to finance welfare measures (see Section 2.3.1) – may have exacerbated the sense of urgency among firms to use available resources rapidly.

20 Training Funds cannot finance OHS training through the collective account, above a certain amount referred to as "*de minimis*".

References

ANPAL (2018), "XVIII Rapporto sulla Formazione Continua", http://www.anpal.gov.it/Dati-e-pubblicazioni/Documents/XVIII-Rapporto-formazione-continua.pdf (accessed on 28 March 2018). [11]

Casano, L. et al. (2017), "Bilateralità e formazione", https://moodle.adaptland.it/mod/book/view.php?id=21892 (accessed on 7 February 2018). [3]

E.Bi.Pro (2017), "Regolament rimborso delle spese sostenute per la formazione in materia di salute e sicurezza nel luogo di lavoro", http://www.ebipro.it/wp-content/uploads/2017/06/Regolamento-CSS.pdf (accessed on 27 March 2018). [22]

European Commission (2017), *Europe's Digital Progress Report (EDPR) 2017, Country Profile Italy*, http://www.agid.gov.it/notizie/2015/03/24/approvati-i-piani-nazionali-. [16]

Fioni, A. (2018), *Quanto valgono le competenze digitali? Gli stipendi ai tempi di industria 4.0.* [17]

Fondimpresa (2017), "Audizione parlamentare", https://www.senato.it/application/xmanager/projects/leg17/attachments/documento_evento_procedura_commissione/files/000/005/416/Memorie_Fondimpresa.pdf (accessed on 29 March 2018). [18]

Fondirigenti (n.d.), "Web survey presso aziende attive", http://www.fondirigenti.it/wp-content/uploads/2015/12/indagineffb7.pdf (accessed on 29 March 2018). [4]

ISTAT (2016), "Cittadini, imprese e ICT", http://www.istat.it/it/files/2016/12/Cittadini-Imprese-e-nuove-tecnologie.pdf?title=Cittadini%2C+imprese+e+ICT+-+21%2Fdic%2F2016+-+Testo+integrale+e+nota+metodologica.pdf (accessed on 10 April 2018). [13]

MISE & MEF (2017), "Piano Nazionale Impresa 4.0", http://www.sviluppoeconomico.gov.it/images/stories/documenti/impresa_40_risultati_2017_azioni_2018.pdf (accessed on 29 March 2018). [20]

Müller, N. and F. Behringer (2012), "Subsidies and Levies as Policy Instruments to Encourage Employer-Provided Training", *OECD Education Working Papers*, No. 80, OECD Publishing, Paris, https://dx.doi.org/10.1787/5k97b083v1vb-en. [23]

OECD (2019), *Getting Skills Right: Making adult learning work in social partnership*, OECD Publishing, Paris. [5]

OECD (2017), *Financial Incentives for Steering Education and Training*, Getting Skills Right, OECD Publishing, Paris, https://dx.doi.org/10.1787/9789264272415-en. [2]

OECD (2017), *Getting Skills Right: Good Practice in Adapting to Changing Skill Needs: A Perspective on France, Italy, Spain, South Africa and the United Kingdom*, Getting Skills Right, OECD Publishing, Paris, https://dx.doi.org/10.1787/9789264277892-en. [25]

OECD (2017), *Getting Skills Right: Italy*, OECD Publishing, Paris, http://dx.doi.org/10.1787/9789264278639-en. [19]

OECD (2017), *Getting Skills Right: Skills for Jobs Indicators*, Getting Skills Right, OECD Publishing, Paris, https://dx.doi.org/10.1787/9789264277878-en. [1]

OECD (2017), *OECD Economic Surveys : Italy 2017*, OECD Publishing, Paris, https://doi.org/10.1787/eco_surveys-ita-2017-en (accessed on 29 March 2018). [14]

OECD (2017), "OECD Skills Strategy Diagnostic Report: Italy", https://www.oecd.org/skills/nationalskillsstrategies/Diagnostic-report-Italy.pdf (accessed on 26 March 2018). [8]

OECD (2016), *Getting Skills Right: Assessing and Anticipating Changing Skill Needs*, OECD Publishing, Paris, http://dx.doi.org/10.1787/9789264252073-en. [7]

OECD (2013), *OECD Skills Outlook 2013: First Results from the Survey of Adult Skills*, OECD Publishing, Paris, https://doi.org/10.1787/9789264204256-en (accessed on 29 March 2018). [15]

Osservatorio (2017), *Industria 4.0: la grande occasione per l'Italia*, https://www.osservatori.net/it_it/osservatori/comunicati-stampa/industria-4.0-la-grande-occasione-per-l-italia (accessed on 5 February 2019). [24]

Socci, M. and A. Principi (2014), "State of the Art of innovative, successful and sustainable approaches to working and learning longer: Lifelong learning National report: ITALY", *Mobilising the Potential of Active Ageing in Europe*, http://mopact.group.shef.ac.uk/wp-content/uploads/2013/10/D3.2-Lifelong-learning-Italian-national-report.pdf (accessed on 9 May 2018). [21]

TUAC (2016), *Unions and Skills: TUAC discussion paper on OECD strategies for skills, Jobs and the Digital Economy.* [6]

UNESCO (2018), *Funding skills development: The private sector contribution*, http://unesdoc.unesco.org/images/0026/002619/261984e.pdf (accessed on 26 June 2018). [12]

UNESCO (2016), *Global report on adult learning*, UNESCO Institute for Lifelong Learning. [10]

Valsega, C. (2017), "Perché è sempre più importante parlare di formazione continua". [9]

Chapter 5. Ensuring that training is of good quality

Ensuring that training is of good quality – e.g. that it is effective, complies with quality standards criteria, and is certified – is fundamental to ensure that available Training Funds resources are put to their best value use. Continuous monitoring of the activities of the Training Funds through good information systems, as well as regular evaluation of the impacts of training on workers' labour market outcomes and firms' performance is essential to keep track of the quality of training. This chapter analyses the mechanisms put in place in Italy to ensure that TF-supported training is of good quality.

5.1. Quality assurance mechanisms

The vast majority of TF-supported training is delivered by non-formal training providers that fall outside the responsibility of standard quality-monitoring institutions.[1] This makes it difficult to monitor the quality of TF-supported training. Indeed, Table 5.1 shows that employers are the main providers of TF-supported training (49.5% of all training plans), followed by training providers/training agencies (23.1%), consultancy and/or training firms (16.3%), while only a very small minority of all training plans are delivered by formal institutions – *e.g.* university (0.5%), private/public educational institutions (0.3%), and public/private research centres (0.2%).

While Training Funds can use different strategies to ensure that the training they finance is of good quality, in general there are no homogeneous training quality standards to which all Training Funds need to comply to. The next sections look at how different quality assurance mechanisms can influence TF-supported training quality, looking particularly at three aspects: (i) accreditation of training providers; (ii) funding allocation procedures; and (iii) monitoring of training providers.

Table 5.1. Providers of TF-supported training, 2016

Providers of TF-supported training	Number of training plans	% of all training plans
Beneficiary enterprise	15 282	49.5
Training provider/training agency	7 143	23.1
Consultancy and/or training firm	5 041	16.3
Other enterprise (not beneficiary)	193	0.6
University	140	0.5
Private/public educational institution	86	0.3
Parent company/controlling undertaking	72	0.2
Private/public research centres	74	0.2
Consortium of beneficiary enterprises	24	0.1
Ecclesiastical institution	32	0.1
Data not available	2 793	9
All providers	29 088	100

1. Data refer to training plans approved between January and December 2016.
2. The question provides multiple answer choices. The sum of the individual answers is used for the calculation of shares.
Source: ANPAL's elaborations based on the Nexus database.

5.1.1. Accreditation of training providers

Each TF has its own accreditation strategy to ensure that funding goes to training providers that are of good quality. Most Training Funds rely on existing regional accreditation systems to select training providers while many Training Funds have developed their own accreditation system.

The lack of a common rule on accreditation procedures, valid for all Training Funds across the whole territory, may bring several challenges. First, it may lead some Training Funds to establish preferential partnerships with training providers, potentially allowing low-quality training providers to obtain Training Funds financing.

Second, it could result in large differences in the quality of training provided across different regions/Training Funds. Indeed, quality criteria vary significantly between regional accreditation systems, and, when in place, between different Training Funds accreditation systems.

Third, such a fragmented approach could also make it difficult for potential participants / firms to compare different programmes and providers, and thus taking informed decisions on which training providers to choose may be challenging.

Another key challenge is that existing accreditation systems (whether regional or developed by Training Funds) often focus on training providers' compliance to formal procedures rather than on the actual quality of the training offered.

While quality is subjective and typically difficult to measure, some Training Funds are currently trying to improve their own accreditation system in a view to embed elements of quality. For example, *Fondimpresa* is planning to adjust its accreditation system so that only training providers that train teachers on a regular basis can receive/keep accreditation. However, this remains quite an isolated practice.

To overcome these challenges, discussions are ongoing on whether Italy should build a national accreditation system – developed and managed by ANPAL – which would develop a set of training quality-standard criteria valid for all training providers. Given the plethora of training providers existing in Italy, the challenge would be to monitor, on a regular basis, that quality criteria are met. The other challenge of adopting a national accreditation system relates to the fact that, at the moment, accreditation of training providers is still under the responsibility of regions.

Perhaps Italy could learn from the experience of OECD countries that have been confronted with similar challenges (OECD, 2019[1]). In France, the Decrée Qualité (adopted in 2017) establishes a set of quality standard criteria to which all training providers need to comply to in order to be able to access funding by training funds (i.e. the OPCA) and other public financing bodies (see Box 5.1).

5.1.2. Funding allocation procedures

Other than accreditation systems, there are also other mechanisms Training Funds can use to ensure that training is of good quality. For example, funding allocation procedures – *i.e.* the selection process through which funding (from collective accounts) is allocated to training proposals/plans – can have crucial implications for training quality.

Again, there is no standard rule and there are large variations in the practices adopted by the Training Funds. Indeed, some Training Funds (e.g. *Foncoop*, *Fondoprofessioni*; *Fondimpresa*) – in a view to minimise conflicts of interests – outsource assessment procedures to external committees, whose members are identified through a careful selection process. Other Training Funds evaluate training plans themselves.

The methodology used for grant allocation also differs across Training Funds. Training Funds typically have two options: (i) **First-come-first-served procedures** (*i.e.* "*avvisi a sportello*"). Training Funds assess whether training proposals meet minimum criteria (previously identified in the grant description) and authorise funding in chronological order of receipt until exhaustion of resource; (ii) **Deadline procedures**. Training Funds establish a deadline after which training proposals are evaluated altogether and then ranked according to quality criteria previously defined.

The methodology used for grant allocation could have huge implications for training quality. For example, the *first-come-first-served* procedure guarantees rapid access to funding (see Section 4.5), but puts less emphasis on quality. The deadline procedure allows Training Funds to reward quality (*e.g.* additional points can be given to training proposals that are innovative, or that draw on SAA exercises to identify firms' skills needs), but at the same time is probably more time-consuming and therefore it could hamper Training Funds' ability to respond quickly to firms' skills needs (see Section 4.5).

Again, Training Funds are free to adopt the strategy they deem most appropriate, reflecting whether they prefer to emphasise responsiveness or training quality. *Fondirigenti*, for example, solely relies on deadline procedures, with a view to steer quality.

Considering the wide variation across Training Funds in the funding allocation procedures adopted, there may be scope for ANPAL to include relevant regulation in the ANPAL Guidelines (see Section 2.3.3 and Annex A). For example, ANPAL Guidelines could make it compulsory for all Training Funds to rely on an external, independent, committee to assess training plans submitted by firms – as already done by some Training Funds.

5.1.3. Monitoring of training providers

Training Funds monitor training programmes mainly through on-spot inspections, *i.e.* to assess whether training has actually taken place. After that TF-supported training has taken place, firms must report on their training activities and there is close monitoring by the Training Funds to ensure that training complies with its guidelines. In cases of deviation, the TF may prescribe corrective actions, e.g. withdrawal from the list of accredited training providers, or withdrawal of the funding.

One key challenge is that – as reported by many stakeholders – monitoring by the Training Funds is often only formal (e.g. it is only meant to establish whether the training has actually taken place), rather than focussed on the quality of the training being delivered.

Another key challenge is that Training Funds typically monitor training financed through collective accounts, while there is no obligation for the Training Funds to monitor training financed through individual accounts.

Finally, some stakeholders report that often there is no follow-up discussion between employees and firms at the end of the training programme. More systematic and structured discussions after training would help both workers and firms to better identify the skills developed during training, and understand how to best apply these skills at work. It would also provide a useful feedback for firms on training's usefulness, effectiveness, and relevance for workers.

Box 5.1. Establishing quality criteria for training providers: the example of France

Since 2014 in France different training financing bodies – including the OPCA, regions, and the Public Employment Service (*Pole Emploi*) – have collaborated to harmonise quality criteria among all training providers.

The fruit of this collaboration was formalised in the *Decrée Qualité*[2], which was introduced in 2015 and came into force in January 2017. The law establishes a set of quality criteria to which training providers need to comply to in order to be able to access financing.

There are a total of 6 criteria – unbundled in 21 different indicators – that revolve around:

- the objectives of training;
- the existence of procedural control mechanisms;
- the adequacy of the pedagogical tools used;
- the quality of teachers;
- the accessibility of information on training offer to the general public;
- the evaluation of training programmes.

A dedicated online platform – the Data Dock (https://www.data-dock.fr/) – allows training providers to register to the system and self-assess against these dimensions. Training providers also need to provide supporting documents that justify their self-assessment for each of the 21 indicators.

A simplified procedure exists for training providers certified by CNEFOP (*Conseil national de l'emploi, de la formation et de l'orientation professionnelles*). After providing proof of certification on the Data Dock, these training providers are exempt from providing documentations in the self-assessment.

Each financing institutions (including OPCA) can chose among the training providers validated in the system and select the training providers they wish to work with.

Source: https://www.data-dock.fr/.

5.2. Strengthening the skills certification system

Skills certification is a formal process through which skills and knowledge (obtained either through formal, non-formal, or informal learning on the job) are validated. Skills certification has several benefits: it can make the outcomes of training participation more visible, transparent, and easily signalled to employers; and may provide further incentives for workers to participate in training.

In recent years, Italy has made significant efforts to create a skills certification system that can be applied consistently across the country. A number of norms[3] have been put in place since 2013 to move from Regional Qualification Frameworks (*Quadri Regionali degli Standard Professionali*) towards a National Qualification Framework (*Quadro*

Nazionale delle Qualificazioni) (OECD, 2017[2]). Today the NQF – officially instituted in January 2018 – applies common skill taxonomy to all regions by creating correspondences between qualifications defined in different RQFs.[4]

Targeted efforts have also been taken to specifically strengthen the role that Training Funds can play in promoting skills certification practices in Italy. In 2012, the so-called Fornero Law (Law 92/2012) identifies Training Funds as potential active players in the Italian skills certification system (Casano et al., 2017[3]).

More recently, the Guidelines instituted by ANPAL in 2018 (see Section 2.3.3.) take further concrete steps to promote the certification of skills obtained through TF-supported training. In particular, the Guidelines adopt a learning outcomes approach, as training plans need to explicitly mention what skills/competences will be developed in order to be eligible for Training Funds funding. Rather than making skills certification compulsory for all TF-supported training – which would be costly and time consuming –, this approach aims to create the conditions for making skills certification easy and possible at any time.

Irrespective of these government's directives, Training Funds (see Box 5.2) and social partners are also taking independent steps to encourage skills certification practices. In 2010, the largest employers' organisation operating in Lombardy (*Assolombarda*), and the largest trade unions (CGIL; CISL; UIL), in collaboration with the Lombardy Region, have joined forces to encourage the certification of skills acquired through TF-sponsored training. In the context of this initiative, social partners have committed to have at least 5% of training plans[5] certified, for example through the regional certification system. As a result of this initiative, between 2012 and 2017, around 17 000 people received Training Funds-sponsored training that led to a certification (Assolombarda, CGIL, CISL, UIL, 2018[4]).

Probably reflecting the good efforts implemented by the government, Training Funds, and social partners, the share of participants to TF-supported training who do not obtain any certification decreased from 51.2% in 2014 to 38.2% in 2016 (

Table 5.2). This drop was mainly driven by an expansion in certifications delivered by regions, training providers and Training Funds.

Despite the progress made, a large share of TF-supported training still remains uncertified. Moreover, even when certification takes place, it is often conducted by different bodies – training providers or Training Funds (42.7%), regions (12%), or other certification bodies (7.2%) – potentially leading to a fragmented system (

Table 5.2). This leaves room to extend certification practices and harmonise the skills certification system further, building on the recent positive developments.

Table 5.2. Certification of skills acquired through TF-supported training

% of participants in TF-supported training, by year

	2014	2015	2016
No certification	**51.2**	**43.9**	**38.2**
Regional certification	3.4	8.2	12
Training provider or TF certification	36.3	40.0	42.7
Other certification	9.1	7.9	7.2
Total	100	100	100

Note: The question provides multiple answer choices. The sum of the individual answers is used for the calculation of shares.
Source: (ANPAL, 2018[5]).

Placing Italy in the international context, evidence from other OECD European countries show that there is large room for improvements. Elaborations of the European Adult Education Survey 2016 show that in Italy only 35% of adults participating in non-formal job-related training received a certificate upon completion, compared to an average of 46% and much below countries such as Poland (69%) and Lithuania (72%) (Figure 5.1).

Figure 5.1. Certification of non-formal learning activities, Italy and European countries, 2016

% of participants in non-formal job-related learning

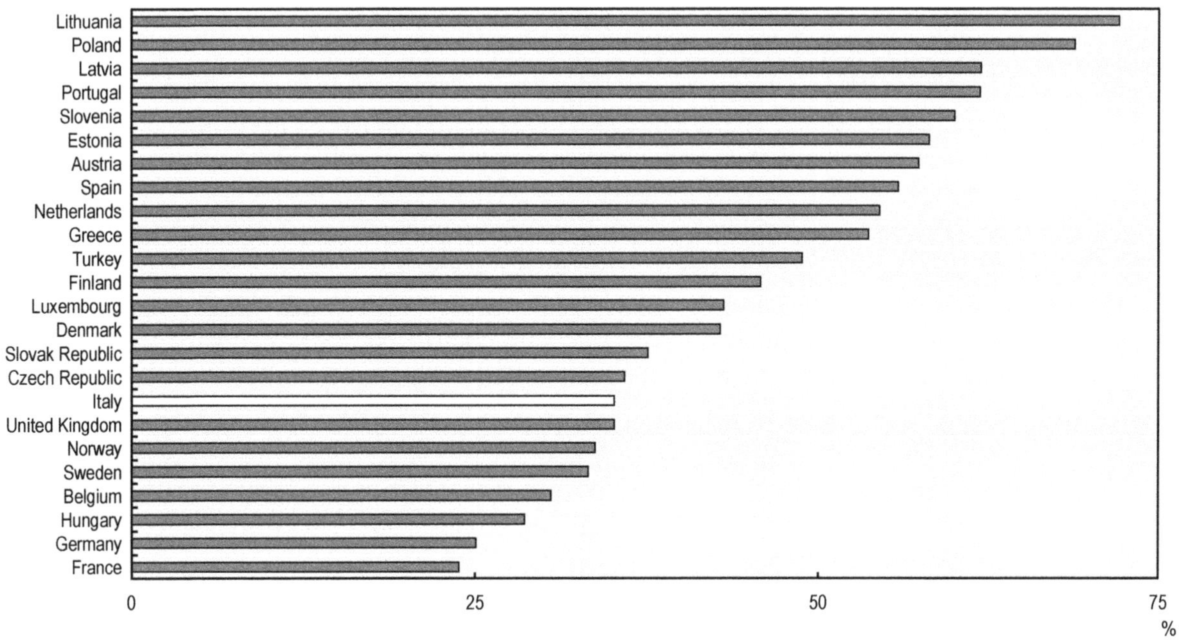

Source: Adult Education survey (AES)

There are many reasons as to why TFs-supported training often continues to remain uncertified, despite all the efforts undertaken by the government, Training Funds, and social partners in recent years. First, in the view of many stakeholders, there seems to be a fundamental incompatibility between regional certification systems and TF-supported training. Indeed, regional certification systems are ill-suited for adults' continuous learning, as they were originally conceived for initial education. For example, regional certification systems typically certify competences associated with "low-skilled" professions, while some categories of high-skilled professions (e.g. in the bank and insurance sector) remain uncovered.

Second, the duration of TF-supported training is typically too short to lead to a full regional certification. Indeed, while legislation allows regional certification for a minimum of twenty-four hours of training, 81.8% of TF-supported training programmes last less than that (see Table 5.3) (ANPAL, 2018[5]).

Table 5.3. Number of hours of TF-supported training

	% of training programmes	Cumulative %
Up to 8 hours	48.7	48.7
From 8 to 16 hours	23.0	71.7
From 16 to 24 hours	10.1	81.8
From 24 to 32 hours	6.8	88.6
From 40 to 48 hours	6.0	94.6
From 48 to 56 hours	1.3	95.9
From 56 to 64 hours	1.0	96.9
From 64 to 72 hours	0.9	97.8
From 72 to 80 hours	0.3	98.1
Over 80 hours	0.5	98.6
Total	100	100

Note: Data includes training programmes approved in 2015 and started in 2016.
Source: ANPAL's elaborations based on the Nexus Database.

Third, TF-supported training plans can cut across (and be delivered in) different regions (*e.g.* in the case of sectoral-level training plans) – making it difficult to effectively use regional certification systems. While the NQF creates a national "taxonomy" which links RQFs with one another, stakeholders claim that correspondences are not always ensured.

Finally, there also seems to be a widespread negative perception around skills certification in Italy, which may discourage workers and firms from undertaking certification procedures. Indeed, skills certification seems to be still considered as a low-status practice, reserved for the low-skilled and/or for workers in low-skilled occupations.

Overall, while it seems unrealistic to expect that every single TF-supported training programme is certified – not least because skills certification takes time, is costly, and certification systems need to be updated frequently to reflect changing skills needs in each profession – more can still be done, building on the significant efforts undertaken in recent years by different actors.

On top of continuing to implement ANPAL Guidelines, going forward it will be important to develop complementary policies with a view to strengthen certification practices further. For example, it could be envisaged to set a minimum training duration, so as to ensure that the (short) length of training courses does not compromise certification. Moreover, each training plan could explicitly refer to a specific skills certification system (e.g. regional; TF certification).

Box 5.2. Good practices in skills certification: examples from Training Funds

Certify skills

In 2010, the *Fondo Banche e Assicurazioni* (FBA), the Training Fund for the banking and insurances sector (hereafter FBA), developed a Commercial Banks Qualifications Inventory. The initiative reflected the inadequacy of the regional certification systems to appropriately define the competences of the banking employees, and was introduced with a view to create synergies with the European Qualification Framework (EQF). The Inventory defines a list of job profiles that encompasses four types of information, namely the job's (i) title (ii) purpose (iii) main responsibilities and activities (iv) and competence profile. In particular, the competence profile lists the knowledge and capabilities required to do the job (Durante, Fraccaroli and Gallo, 2015[6]). The project was led by FBA and the Italian Banking Association (ABI), it proactively involved banks and trade union representatives of the banking industry, and received the technical support of the then-ISFOL (now-INAPP). Building on the Inventory, today FBA is accredited[6] to certify 32 different job profiles and offers the possibility to certify skills for free. So far, around 1 000 employees of the banking sector have obtained certification by FBA. Because the Inventory is also linked to the EQF, the certification is recognised in other European countries, and is valid for a period of 3 to 5 years depending on the job profile (Masiello, n.d.[7]).

Reward skills certification

Some Training Funds (e.g. *Fondimpresa, Fon.coop*), provide higher scores to training plans that foresee skills certification after training completion.

Subsidise the cost associated with certification

Some Training Funds subsidise the cost associated with certification procedures - a practice also implemented in training funds in other OECD countries, e.g. the Netherlands.[7] For example, *Fon.coop* (e.g. through Grant 35) requires that at least 30% of resources are devoted to activities other than training, including workers' skills certification.

Develop training programmes following a learning outcomes approach

Another good example is the "SMART CARD Competenze", carried out since 2015 by *Fondo Formazione PMI (FAPI)*. This is a skills certification instrument through which training providers can submit training proposals broken down in "skills units" as defined in RQFs (ANPAL, 2018[5]). A support service system has been put in place to help training providers navigate the new process.

5.3. Fostering a healthy competitive environment among Training Funds

Training Funds are in competition with one another. Their lack of direct linkages to economic sectors[8], combined with the principle of "portability", means that firms are allowed to enrol in the Training Fund of their choosing and/or switch to a different Training Fund virtually at any time. As an illustration, it is interesting to observe how some of the newer Training Funds[9] are increasing their catchment area not much by reaching out to firms outside of the Training Funds system, but rather by attracting firms already enrolled in other, older, Training Funds (ANPAL, 2018[5]).[10] For example, *Fonarcom* (established in 2006) is today the second largest Training Fund in Italy for number of firms enrolled, after *Fondimpresa* (established in 2002).

While in theory, a certain amount of competition is desirable as it may push Training Funds to improve the quality of their services, in practice this does not happen. Many Training Funds try to attract firms by easing administrative procedures rather than by focussing on quality.

There are several reasons as to why this may happen. First, some firms (especially SMEs that struggle to articulate their skill needs) show little interest in training and may pay little attention to the quality of courses offered (see Chapter 3).

Second, in smaller firms, training decisions (including on what Training Funds to choose) are often outsourced to external business consultants (Casano et al., 2017[3]) who, however, are not always fully aware of the firm's skills needs and may orient their decisions based on administrative (rather than skills needs) considerations.

In the past, weak implementation of portability rules[11] and a blurry legal framework[12] also played a role in shaping an unhealthy competitive environment, although the Guidelines established by ANPAL in 2018 (see Chapter 2 and Annex A) already take steps to address these challenges. For example, the Guidelines make the rules around portability stricter and clearer, and update the legal framework legislation in a view to make all Training Funds play by a clear, and shared, set of rules.

Going forward, there are additional policy options that the government could explore to promote virtuous competition patterns among Training Funds and ultimately improve training quality. It is worth noting, however, that the international experience is inconclusive in this respect: countries adopts very different approaches, there is no one-fits-all solution and each approach has its strengths and weaknesses:

- **Reduce the number of Training Funds**, for example by merging some of the smaller or less performing Training Funds. This option – which has already been proposed by various actors (Casano et al., 2017[3]) – would generate economies of scales, reduce overall administrative costs, on top of giving enrolled firms an opportunity of interaction with a wider platform of firms. On the other hand, however, it may imply looser relationships between Training Funds and firms. In the international context, there is no ideal number of training funds, and practices vary considerably across countries, going from one national training fund, e.g. in Spain, to about 132 training funds in the Netherlands. Some countries, however, have taken steps to streamline the system and reduce the number of funds in recent years. In France, for example, in 2009 the number of training funds was reduced from around 96 to 20 (Podevin et al., 2018[8])
- **Link each Training Fund to an economic sector**, bringing the levy back to its original objectives.[13] This policy option would make it easier for social partners to agree on a shared training strategy based on common training needs. On the downside, there is a risk to invest solely in skills that are too sector-specific, thereby limiting workers' cross-sectoral mobility and investments in transversal skills (OECD, 2017[9]).[14] Again, different countries adopt different approaches. In some countries training funds are linked to economic sectors (e.g. Belgium, Ireland, the Netherlands, South Africa), in other countries they are cross-sectoral

(e.g. Finland, Greece, Hungary, Poland), while other countries have both types of training funds coexist (e.g. Norway, France).

- **Set minimum operational standards**, against which each Training Fund could be regularly assessed in order to continue operating. Minimum standards could include quantitative indicators (e.g. number of workers served or amount of EUR collected) as well as qualitative ones. However, quality is typically harder to define and certainly more difficult to monitor. The international experience shows that while some countries do set minimum operational standards – e.g. France, where each training fund (OPCA) needs to collect a minimum amount of financial resources (EUR 100 million) in order to continue operating – this is not systematically done in all countries with a levy scheme in place.

5.4. Strengthening information systems

Collecting information on the activities of the Training Funds is fundamental to monitor who is benefiting from training and who is being left behind, understand where resources are being invested, and keep track of progress.

The Nexus database is the ad-hoc information system conceived to regularly collect data on the activities of the Training Funds. Operative since 2008, the Nexus database was previously managed by INAPP and is now under the aegis of ANPAL.

It collects valuable information on a regular basis (every six months) from all Training Funds. The information collected mainly focusses on training plans (e.g. number of participants, objectives of the training, financial resources allocated), individual training programmes (e.g. thematic areas, modality of training delivery, certification), as well as the beneficiaries of training (firms and workers).

The data collected through the Nexus database are disseminated in a statistical report on continuous learning (*Rapporto Sulla Formazione Continua*) – which is published on a yearly basis by ANPAL.[15]

Despite being an essential tool to ensure that standard information is collected across all Training Funds on a regular basis, the database has several limitations that need to be addressed:

- No information is collected at the individual (worker) and firm level (the unit of analysis is the individual training plan). Designed this way, the database can generate double counting, making it difficult to extract the actual number of participants or the number of firms involved in training, or to analyse training participation dynamics by individual and firm characteristics (Casano et al., 2017[3]).
- Information feeds into the database in scattered ways. For example, information sometimes refers to previous semesters/years. [16] This can significantly bias the results (and explain why data sometimes vary significantly from one year to the next) and ultimately undermine data elaborations (ANPAL, 2018[5]).
- Some aspects of the activities of the Training Funds are currently overlooked. For example, there is no information on the quality of training provided, or on the financing channels used to sponsor training (e.g. collective vs individual accounts) (Casano et al., 2017[3]). A similar challenge is that data is collected at a high level of aggregation. To give one example, while the database collects

information on certification, it only captures whether the certification has taken place and by what entity it was carried out (e.g. region; Training Fund; training providers; or other private entities) (see section 5.2). Going forward, information could be collected at a higher level of disaggregation, for example on the type of competences certified. To give another example, there are only 14 "thematic areas" included in the Nexus database. Going forward, the number of thematic areas could be increased. This would allow Training Funds to be more precise on the type of skills their training aims to develop; and at the same time will allow policy makers/researchers to better understand of what skills are being developed through Training Funds.

- There is limited communication with other existing information systems. For instance, the Nexus database does not communicate with regional information systems, or with the stand-alone information system developed by Forma.temp – the Training Fund dedicated to temporary agency workers.

The government is already taking steps to address some of these challenges. ANPAL is planning to create an integrated information system on continuous learning, which should collect information on individuals' training financed either entirely or partially by public resources (*e.g.* by Training Funds; regions), and will be able to follow workers among different training programmes, jobs and employment statuses. Not only would this integrated system shed further light on workers' training attitudes, but it would also allow policy makers to monitor co-ordination and duplication of training actions.

Another step in the right direction is the new obligation – imposed through the ANPAL Guidelines (see Section 2.3.3) – that Training Funds provide anonymised information at the individual worker level. This information will significantly strengthen the data elaboration capacity of the Nexus database and ultimately improve monitoring.

Going forward, in order to improve the current information system and make it more responsive to users' needs, it will be important to establish more systematic opportunities for dialogue between the different actors involved in the Nexus database, including Training Funds, ANPAL, INPS, regions. One option worth exploring would be to establish a forum for discussion managed and led by a *National Observatory for Adult Learning* (see Section 6.1).

5.5. Evaluating the impact of training on firms and workers' performance

Impact evaluation analysis can shed light on the benefits associated with training, e.g. on firm's performance, or workers' wages. The results could encourage firms to provide more training to their employees, and increase workers' incentives to participate in training[17]. Impact evaluation could also help Training Funds redirect resources to the most effective interventions, which is crucial in the context of tight budgets (see Chapter 2), as well as allow Training Funds to scale-up successful pilots and terminate unsuccessful ones.

Training Funds can directly evaluate the quality of the training they sponsor, for example by asking training participants and firms to express their views on the effectiveness and usefulness of training. *Fondimpresa*, for example, has established a research centre that evaluates the impact of training on various aspects of workers' and firms' performances, both at the national and regional level. For instance, the evaluation sheds light on participants' satisfaction and perceptions of the usefulness of training. The research centre also conducts surveys of firms' satisfaction, *e.g.* looking at whether training has improved workers' skills, efficiency, output quality, and ability to integrate the work environment (Fondimpresa (2016[10]); (2018[11]).

Training Funds can also outsource the impact evaluation analysis to external, independent, evaluators. At least three examples can be highlighted:

- *Fondirigenti* has recently promoted a study – conducted by the University of Trento, and published by the "Industrial Relations" review of Berkeley University – on the returns to investment in training for middle-managers on firms' performance. The study shows that, among medium and large firms, a 1 percentage point increase in training hours leads to an increase of total factor productivity of about 0.12%. Results for small firms are positive but not statistically significant (Feltrinelli, Gabriele and Trento, 2017[12]).
- *Fon.coop* in cooperation with the Sapienza University has started a process of evaluation of one of its grants (i.e. Grant 35). The evaluation – qualitative in nature – aims to identify the factors that have favoured (and hampered) the effectiveness of the grant, and whether the grant has obtained its objectives. The research (conducted between 2017 and 2018) represents a first evaluation model that will pave the way for future and more systematic evaluation analysis conducted by the Training Fund.
- *Fondimpresa*, in collaboration with INAPP, has started a pilot project to evaluate the impact of learning on participants and firms. The pilot collects quantitative data and case studies on firms that have benefited from training financed by *Fondimpresa* in the period 2016-2017. The pilot project will be scaled up and cover a larger number of firms through online platform questionnaires.

Notwithstanding interesting initiatives autonomously undertaken by Training Funds, various observers agree that what is still missing in Italy is a *systematic* effort to evaluate the impact of sponsored training, conducted on a regular basis across all Training Funds, and preferably by an independent and objective research body.

Indeed, while the above-mentioned initiatives undertaken by Training Funds are extremely important to shed some light on the benefits of learning and the effectiveness of training programmes – they are still conducted on an ad-hoc basis. Moreover, they may create a fragmented picture where different aspects of learning are evaluated, and results are rarely comparable with one another.

Italy is not alone in this challenge. Rigorous evaluations of the effectiveness of levy programmes are extremely uncommon among countries that have training funds in place. Analysis are mostly limited to comparison of outputs and targets (e.g. related to the number of persons trained) (Müller and Behringer, 2012[13]; Cedefop, 2008[14]; UNESCO, 2018[15]).

However, some useful international good practices exist. In Ireland, for example, an independent evaluation of the activities of *Skillnet* programmes is carried out every year. The evaluation, which is supported by extensive new primary research, stakeholder engagement and detailed analysis, includes a particular focus on assessing the alignment of activities with the requirements of the National Training Fund, including the need to ensure value for money in the utilisation of public resources (Indecon International Economic Consultants, 2017[16]).

What is encouraging is that Italy already possesses the technical capacity to conduct systematic impact evaluation analysis, e.g. INAPP and/or ANPAL would be well placed to take on this function. Moreover, Italy could also build on the experience of the European Social Fund, which is very demanding in terms of ex-ante, *in itinere*, and ex-post evaluation, and for which a robust monitoring procedure has been put in place to carefully assess the outcomes of programmes.[18]

Concerted efforts to go in this direction will be crucial in the future. A *National Observatory for Adult Learning* (see Section 6.1) could coordinate or at least support a more systematic effort to evaluate and assess the effectiveness of TF-supported training.

Notes

[1] For example, the quality of the university system is monitored by ANVUR (National agency for the evaluation of the university and research system). The quality of Provincial Centres for Adult Education (CPIA) is monitored by INVALSI (National institute for the evaluation of the education system).

[2] Decree n° 2015-790 of June 30th 2015

[3] The Law 13/2013 and the Inter-Ministerial Degree 30 June 2015.

[4] See the Atlante del Lavoro e delle Qualificazioni: http://atlantelavoro.inapp.org/.

[5] Expressed in number of training hours.

[6] By Accredia – the Italian Accreditation Body (*Ente Italiano di Accreditamento*).

[7] This is what happens, for example, in some OECD countries – e.g. the Netherlands (OECD, 2017[9]) - where certification procedures are directly financed by training funds.

[8] Today, in fact, most of the Training Funds are delinked to a specific economic sector. There are some notable exceptions: For.Agri (agriculture sector), Fondo Banche e Assicurazioni (bank sector), Fond.ER (religious bodies) and Fondoprofessioni (professional firms).

[9] I.e. Training Funds created after 2008.

[10] These "new" Training Funds are becoming increasingly important: from 2011 to 2016, firms' enrolment rates passed from 12.2% to 33.7% (Casano et al., 2017[3]). And while the share of resources managed by the new Training Funds is limited – reflecting the fact that they attract many SMEs that contribute little due to a smaller workforce – it is still increasing: from 2014 to 2017 the share of resources managed by these "new" Training Funds grew from 8.9% to 13.5% (ANPAL, 2018[5]).

[11] The principle of portability – which in theory should pave the way for a healthy competitive system – was not working well, at least before the implementation of the ANPAL Guidelines. Indeed, many firms are not eligible. The rule does not apply to firms with less than 50 employees and/or firms with an annual turnover of less than EUR 10 million, and applies only when the firm can transfer at least EUR 3 000), and the rule is weakly implemented. As already highlighted by the Italian Competition Authority (AGCM), in the past years some Training Funds have tried to obstruct or delay portability, for example by developing ad-hoc internal rules which in practice limited implementation (Autorità Garante della Concorrenza e del Mercato, 2016[17]). As other examples: some Training Funds have missed the deadlines normally permitted by the law to follow up on firms' request for mobility. In other occasions, Training Funds have burdened firms with additional requests for documentation, as a way to delay portability.

[12] The blurry legal framework which has regulated the activities of the Training Funds for around 15 years favoured the use of practices of ambiguous legitimacy. For example, in 2016 the Italian Competition Authority (AGCM) pointed to the lack of transparency and accountability in the way some Training Funds allocated funding (Autorità Garante della Concorrenza e del Mercato, 2016[17]).

[13] The article 48 of the 388/2000 Law contemplated the possibility to create Training Funds for each economic sector of industry, agriculture, and tertiary services and manufacturing (Casano et al., 2017[3]).

[14] Indeed, one key challenge in the Netherlands is that training funds do not sufficiently support the reallocation of skilled workers across sectors and develop skills that are too firm-specific.

[15] Until 2017, the report was managed by ISFOL – now-INAPP.

[16] The late registration of certain training plans into the information system can be due to two main reasons: (i) data feeds into the information system only once training plans are concluded, even for multi-annual training plans which are typically concluded years after their approval; (ii) information on training plans is sometimes corrected after quality checks, in a view to improve the qualify of the information system.

[17] This is particularly important in the Italian context where – as discussed in Chapter 3 – there is little information available on the benefits of learning, and many workers – especially the most disadvantaged – lack motivation to participate.

[18] Some local authorities have established Regional Offices to monitor and assess Labour and Vocational Training Policies. For instance, the Istituto Regionale Programmazione economica della Toscana (IRPET) carries out periodical evaluation of labour market and vocational training policies in Toscana Region.

References

ANPAL (2018), "XVIII Rapporto sulla Formazione Continua", http://www.anpal.gov.it/Dati-e-pubblicazioni/Documents/XVIII-Rapporto-formazione-continua.pdf (accessed on 28 March 2018). [5]

Assolombarda, CGIL, CISL, UIL (2018), *Il Lavoro a Milano*. [4]

Autorità Garante della Concorrenza e del Mercato (2016), *Bollettino*, http://www.agcm.it/component/joomdoc/bollettini/15-16.pdf/download.html (accessed on 9 May 2018). [17]

Casano, L. et al. (2017), "Bilateralità e formazione", https://moodle.adaptland.it/mod/book/view.php?id=21892 (accessed on 7 February 2018). [3]

Cedefop (2008), "Sectoral Training Funds in Europe", *CEDEFOP*. [14]

Durante, G., A. Fraccaroli and G. Gallo (2015), *Manual for the Certification of Commercial Banks Qualifications According to the European Qualifications Framework (EQF) Principles*, Fondo Banche Assicurazioni, https://www.bancariaeditrice.it/download/GetDownloadSfogliatore/2Cllr0dIJuMZvOkqIu2HbFrseMMvTwcZrXOSc5zT5MvlSN4kIxeS (accessed on 9 May 2018). [6]

Feltrinelli, E., R. Gabriele and S. Trento (2017), "The Impact of Middle Manager Training on Productivity: A Test on Italian Companies", *Industrial Relations*, http://dx.doi.org/10.1111/irel.12174. [12]

Fondimpresa (2018), *Rapporto sulle attività di monitoraggio valutativo: anno 2017*. [11]

Fondimpresa (2016), "Rapporto sulle attività di monitoraggio valutativo - anno 2016", http://www.fondimpresa.it/images/in_cifre/monitoraggi/26_06_2017/rapporto_monitoraggio_valutativo_2016_Avviso_5-2013.pdf (accessed on 30 March 2018). [10]

Indecon International Economic Consultants (2017), *Evaluation of Skillnets*, https://www.skillnetireland.ie/wp-content/uploads/2018/04/evaluation_skillnets_programmes_2016.pdf (accessed on 27 June 2018). [16]

Masiello, A. (n.d.), *Professione bancario: valutazione e certificazione delle qualifiche*, http://archivio.firstcisl.it/nazionale/documenti/testo-articolo-1 (accessed on 9 May 2018). [7]

Müller, N. and F. Behringer (2012), "Subsidies and Levies as Policy Instruments to Encourage Employer-Provided Training", *OECD Education Working Papers*, No. 80, OECD Publishing, Paris, https://dx.doi.org/10.1787/5k97b083v1vb-en. [13]

OECD (2019), *Getting Skills Right: Future-Ready Adult Learning Systems*, Getting Skills Right, OECD Publishing, Paris, https://dx.doi.org/10.1787/9789264311756-en. [1]

OECD (2017), *Getting Skills Right: Italy*, OECD Publishing, Paris, http://dx.doi.org/10.1787/9789264278639-en. [2]

OECD (2017), "OECD Skills Strategy Diagnostic Report: The Netherlands", https://www.oecd.org/skills/nationalskillsstrategies/OECD-Skills-Strategy-Diagnostic-Report-Netherlands.pdf (accessed on 31 March 2018). [9]

Podevin, G. et al. (2018), *Transformation des OPCA au fil des réformes récentes : vers un nouveau modèle économique ?*, CÉREQ ÉTUDES. [8]

UNESCO (2018), *Funding skills development: The private sector contribution*, http://unesdoc.unesco.org/images/0026/002619/261984e.pdf (accessed on 26 June 2018). [15]

Chapter 6. Enhancing coordination among different actors

Each Training Fund operates in a complex adult learning system, where different actors are responsible for delivering different types of adult learning programmes. Within this context, in order to ensure that training programmes reach all adults (including the unemployed), are mutually reinforcing, and do not overlap, it is important that Training Funds do not work in silos but work effectively together, with other actors involved in adult learning, as well as with the government. This chapter analyses what mechanisms are in place to enhance coordination across different actors involved in adult learning.

6.1. Improving coordination between Training Funds and other actors involved in adult learning

In the views of many stakeholders, one key challenge of the Training Funds system in Italy is lack of coordination. Too often, Training Funds work in silos and communication is unstructured both (i) across Training Funds, (ii) between Training Funds and other actors involved in adult learning (CPIAs; PESs; regions), and (iii) between Training Funds and the government.

Interactions across Training Funds remain most often ad-hoc, informal, and largely dependent on the goodwill of management board members, with little institutional/formal opportunity to meet on a systematic basis. This means that there are little opportunities for dialogue, cooperation, and sharing of good practices across Training Funds.

That being said, sporadic examples of coordination across Training Funds exist. One good practice is the initiative promoted by CGIL, one of the largest trade unions in Italy. Since 2017, CGIL has started bringing together CGIL member unionists involved in adult learning, including unionists in Training Funds' management boards and in the regions (Coordinamento Fondi Interprofessionali Cgil Nazionale, forthcoming[1]). The objective of the initiative is to improve coordination among CGIL members, enhance the influence of CGIL in the development of training programmes, and ultimately improve the effectiveness of trade unions' involvement in adult learning. In particular, CGIL has started carrying out two types of activities: (i) organise regular seminars – roughly on a monthly basis – around important topics such as skills certification, the national qualification framework, and the implications of new legal frameworks (e.g. the Law of State Aids, the ANPAL Guidelines) for the activities of the Training Funds; and (ii) conduct research studies that investigate how the role of trade unions has evolved in supporting the activities of the Training Funds. This initiative is a very welcome step in the right direction, that in the future could potentially be scaled-up to all Training Funds regardless of their trade unions affiliation.

Another – and related – policy option worth exploring would be to develop an electronic coordination platform dedicated to all Training Funds, with the aim to facilitate cooperation and discussion. In this respect, Italy could perhaps learn from the experience of the Netherlands, where training funds have established a coordination platform that provides them with an opportunity to share good practices, develop joint projects, and meet on a regular basis. As of today, 26 out of the 132 training funds currently operational in the Netherlands are part of the platform, including the largest training funds.

Coordination between Training Funds and other actors involved in adult learning (e.g. CPIA, PES, regions) is also important to limit overlap/duplication of interventions – which is fundamental in the context of limited budgets – and ensure that training opportunities reach everybody and are inclusive (see Chapter 3). Indeed, TF-supported training could be used to reach the target groups and/or develop the skills that are typically not reached/developed by other actors involved in adult learning.

Despite the potential benefits of coordination, at the moment there are little linkages between Training Funds and CPIA (*Centri Provinciali per l'Istruzione degli Adulti*), or between Training Funds and Public Employment Services (*centri per l'impiego*). And while Training Funds and regions do coordinate in some instances, dialogue takes place on an ad-hoc basis and is mainly limited to the sharing of information,[1] and sometimes co-programming of grants.[2]

Systematic coordination with government institutions is also important as it could help Training Funds better participate in the policy dialogue and ensure that their concerns and priorities are reflected in the policy agenda. Examples of good practices can already be highlighted. For example, the Ministry of Education (MIUR) and the Training Fund *FonArcom* have recently signed an agreement to reinforce the collaboration between the education system and the world of work (MIUR and Fonarcom, 2016[2]). Among the measures agreed upon, *FonArcom* has commited to finance training programmes in firms engaged in the implementation of *Alternanza Scuola Lavoro* – i.e. a compulsory work-based learning scheme targeted to all upper-secondary students, implemented in the context of the *Buona Scuola Reform* put in place by the Ministry of Education (MIUR).

While positive examples of cooperation do exist, more needs to be done in this area to make interactions with the government less scattered and more structured. While a National Observatory on Adult Learning (*Osservatorio Nazionale sulla Formazione Continua*) was established by the MLPS[3] in 2003 for a period of three years, its mandate was never renewed and thus the Observatory is currently not operational.[4] While several regional observatories on continuous learning have emerged since[5], going forward one important possibility to enhance co-operation and co-ordination of training provision in Italy would be to re-establish the National Observatory on Adult Learning, building on the initiative already initiated 15 years ago. The Observatory could involve representatives from the MLPS, regions, INAPP, and Training Funds – and could be led by ANPAL. The Observatory could have different roles, including organising regular meetings to discuss important topics such as skills needs, improvements in the information systems, skills certification. Moreover, the Observatory could develop a national adult learning strategy – still lacking in Italy – and ensure that the activities of the Training Funds are well aligned to the skills priorities identified at the national level.

In a similar vein, the government could create a dedicated department in the MLPS that deals exclusively with Training Funds, along the line of what has already been implemented in other countries with a training levy in place. In South Africa, for example, the Department for Higher Education and Training has set up a Directorate – the SETA Coordination Directorate – specifically designed for interfacing with training funds (so-called SETAs), monitoring their activities, and organising regular meeting points.

6.2. Expanding Training Funds' responsibilities towards the unemployed

Training Funds are increasingly called upon to play a greater role in the delivery of active labour market policies, and expand beyond their traditional target population (the employed) towards the unemployed, the inactive, and workers at risk of dismissal. Since the inception of the economic crisis, Training Funds have been proactively taking steps in this direction. For example:

- *Fondimpresa*, upon derogation by the MLPS, in 2010 has devoted EUR 50 million to the re-training of redundancy workers (*lavoratori in mobilità*) to enhance their employability and facilitate their transition to work. On top of financing the training, *Fondimpresa* – together with social partners and training providers – also played another important role: it identified the firms that were willing to hire the redundancy worker, and financed training that responded to their needs; or, when this was not possible, identified the skills needs of the territory, financed training that responded to such needs, and assisted the trained redundancy workers with their job search. The initiative was very successful, with over 55% of beneficiaries finding a job after training (Fondimpresa, 2013[3]).

These results are remarkable especially when considering that that PES typically manage to place only 3% of unemployed people after a training programme (Casano et al., 2017[4]).

- *Foncoop* developed dedicated training grants[6] targeted to firms with workers receiving social safety nets. Priority was given to training projects presented by firms with vulnerable workers, namely women, workers over 45, or low-skilled youth.[7]
- *Fondirigenti* has recently destined EUR 800 thousand to managers who are involuntary unemployed and registered in the PES. *Fondirigenti* also has established an unemployment agency that collects the profiles of managers looking for jobs, in a view to retrain them and support their transition to jobs.
- Other Training Funds (e.g. *Fondimpresa*) finance training of newly hired employees or unemployed/inactive people (provided that the firm hires the person after completion of training). *Fonarcom* is considering putting in place the grant "Forma e Ricolloca" (Train and Relocate) that finances training for firms taking on unemployed people. The training must last at least 40 hours of which 20 after a job contract is signed.

These initiatives show the engagement of Training Funds to go beyond their initial mission and play a more proactive role in the re-integration of unemployed people in the labour market and, more broadly, in the delivery of ALMPs.

What happens in Italy is not too different from what can be observed in other OECD countries with a levy system in place, where the role of the training funds has been expanding to help address the challenges brought about the economic crisis. In France, for example, training funds (*i.e.* OPCA) can contribute to financing training for new hires (previously unemployed registered in the PES) with the aim of closing the gap between the skills possessed by the new hire and the skills required in their new job (OECD, 2017[5]). In Ireland, while the focus of the Skillnet training networks lies in upgrading the skills of the employees of participating enterprises, many networks also provide training to unemployed workers under a programme separately funded by Skillnets Ireland – Job-seekers Support Programme (JSSP). JSSP training courses and work placements are solely for people that are unemployed, and in areas where Irish companies have skill gaps/needs.

It is noteworthy that in the Italian case these efforts remain ad-hoc and very much dependant on individual initiatives of Training Funds. The bulk of training programmes remain focussed on permanent and temporary workers (either full- or part-time), which absorb 87% of all TF-supported training programmes, while only 0.2% of training programmes are devoted to workers on safety nets or redundancy workers (see Figure 6.1 and Table 6.1).

Going forward, if the Training Funds have to start playing a more concrete role in the re-skilling of the unemployed and the delivery of ALMPs, there is a need to update the legal framework so as to ensure that the new responsibilities are reflected in the legislation.

Some steps in this direction have already been taken and the legal framework has recently been updated to ensure that Training Funds can play a bigger role in training the unemployed population. In particular:

- The Jobs Act includes the Training Funds in the "*Rete dei servizi e delle misure di politica attiva del lavoro*" (network for the provision of active labour market policies), paving the way for better cooperation between Training Funds and the PESs in the delivery of ALMPs.

- With the Jobs Act, Training Funds are also asked to contribute to the development of the "personalised service pact" (*patto di servizio personalizzato*) – an action plan stipulated between the unemployed and the PES aimed at improving the employability of the unemployed through several measures, including training.
- According to the Jobs Act, Training Funds should also cooperate in the activation of unemployment benefit recipients.
- More recently, the 2018 Budget Law extends the relocation allowance (*assegno di ricollocazione*) – previously only targeted to long-term unemployed (over four months) – to other categories of workers, namely employees of firms undergoing structural changes, and workers in the special lay-off fund (*Cassa Integrazione*). According to the recent law, Training Funds resources can be used to finance training for this category of workers.

While these adjustments are steps in the right direction, it remains unclear how they will be implemented in practice. For example, the network for the provision of active labour market policies is not yet operative, and therefore it will be important to monitor how, concretely, Training Funds will cooperate with other actors for the delivery of ALMPs.

It is also unclear how Training Funds will reach out to unemployment benefit recipients, considered that most Training Funds lack the necessary territorial structures to successfully perform these tasks (Casano, 2018[6]).

Extending Training Funds' outreach towards the unemployed will also require additional financial resources. As discussed in Chapter 2, the resources available to the Training Funds are already limited, and it is unrealistic to expect Training Funds to perform new functions without additional resources.

Another key concern is that Training Funds will now have to align to the strategic objectives established by the Ministry of Labour in the field of ALMPs. In the views of several observers, this could potentially reduce Training Funds' autonomy in setting skills priorities, a responsibility that was, up to now, reserved to social partners (Casano, 2015[7]; Eurofound, 2016[8]).

Figure 6.1. TF-supported training programme, by type of workers' contracts, 2008-2015 and 2016

% of all programmes, 2016

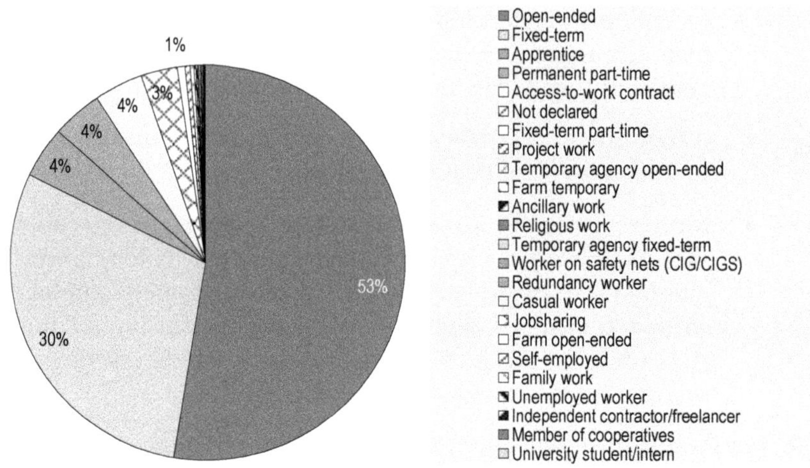

Source: ANPAL's elaborations based on the Nexus database.ANPAL Guidelines.

Table 6.1. TF-supported training programme, by type of workers' contracts, 2008-2015 and 2016

Number of programmes and % of all programmes, 2008-2015 and 2016

	Number of programmes	% of all programmes	Number of programmes	% of all programmes
Type of contract	2008-2015	2008-2015	2016	2016
Open-ended	**3 690 438**	**51.0**	**206 456**	**52.6**
Fixed-term	**1 904 343**	**26.3**	**116 512**	**29.7**
Permanent part-time,	**849 906**	**11.8**	**16 156**	**4.1**
Fixed-term part-time	**106 135**	**1.5**	**2 496**	**0.6**
Access-to-work contract	377 848	5.2	16 058	4.1
Apprentice	91 706	1.3	16 576	4.2
Project work	14 174	0.2	1 588	0.4
Temporary agency open-ended	18 963	0.3	1 235	0.3
Farm temporary	5 642	0.1	630	0.2
Ancillary work	358	0.0	463	0.1
Religious work	8 615	0.1	453	0.1
Temporary agency fixed-term	6 640	0.1	442	0.1
Worker on safety nets (CIG/CIGS)	**13 974**	**0.2**	**393**	**0.1**
Redundancy worker	**1 493**	**0.0**	**342**	**0.1**
Casual worker	2 743	0.0	331	0.1
Jobsharing	26 253	0.4	197	0.1
Farm open-ended	2 631	0.0	186	0.0
Self-employed	305	0.0	127	0.0
Family work	833	0.0	112	0.0
Unemployed worker	205	0.0	8	0.0
Independent contractor/freelancer	21	0.0	0	0.0
Member of cooperatives	88	0.0	0	0.0
University student/intern	53	0.0	0	0.0
Not declared	106 765	1.5	11 754	3.0

Source: ANPAL's elaborations based on the Nexus database.ANPAL Guidelines.

Notes

[1] Training Funds have to communicate their training plans to regions, which in turn can take them into account into their planning strategies (see Law 289/2002). This can help regions channel resources to target groups, and skills, typically not covered by Training Funds.

[2] In some virtuous cases, Training Funds and regions co-programme grants. For example, in 2015 FonArCom and the region Valle D'Aosta jointly developed and financed a training grant of EUR 300 thousands, targeted to temporary workers of Training Funds-member firms (ISFOL, 2017[9]). Other examples of grant co-design exist between Regione Lombardia and certain Training Funds (*i.e.* Fondartigianato, Fon.coop) (Fondimpresa, 2018[10]).

[3] DM 383/V/03. See http://www.fondir.it/sites/default/files/normativa/DM_383.PDF.

[4] The Observatory included representatives from the MLPS, regions, employers' organisations, trade unions, and benefited from the technical assistance of the then-ISFOL (now-INAPP) – and its responsibilities involved setting the strategic priorities of the Training Funds and monitor Training Funds activities.

[5] Several regional observatories on continuous learning are in place in Italy (*e.g.* Lombardia, Piemonte, Toscana) which aim to monitor adult learning activities and strengthen collaboration among different actors, including Training Funds, in a view to rationalise financial resources (Casano et al., 2017[4]).

[6] e.g. Avviso 28.

[7] Under 29 with at best upper secondary education.

References

Casano, L. (2018), "Ripensare i Fondi Interprofessionali per la formazione continua: uno sguardo ai progetti di riforma francesi", *Adapt*, http://www.bollettinoadapt.it/wp-content/uploads/2018/03/Ripensare-i-Fondi-Interprofessionali-per-la-formazione-continua-uno-sguardo-ai-progetti-di-riforma-francesi.pdf (accessed on 26 March 2018). [6]

Casano, L. (2015), "Jobs Act e Fondi Paritetici Interprofessionali per la formazione continua", *Adapt*. [7]

Casano, L. et al. (2017), "Bilateralità e formazione", https://moodle.adaptland.it/mod/book/view.php?id=21892 (accessed on 7 February 2018). [4]

Coordinamento Fondi Interprofessionali Cgil Nazionale (forthcoming), *Fondi Paritetici Interprofessionali: una scommessa aperta*. [1]

Eurofound (2016), "Vocational training paritarian institutions", https://www.eurofound.europa.eu/printpdf/observatories/emcc/erm/support-instrument/vocational-training-paritarian-institutions (accessed on 3 April 2018). [8]

Fondimpresa (2018), *La formazione continua e gli interventi finanziati da Fondimpresa Anno 2015 -Lombardia*, http://www.fondimpresa.it/images/Ufficio_Studi_e_Ricerche/Report_2015/Rapporto-AT-Lombardia.pdf (accessed on 10 May 2018). [10]

Fondimpresa (2013), *Dal Fondo in Poi. Storie di rinascita in tempo di crisi*. [3]

ISFOL (2017), "Rapporto sulla Formazione Continua in Italia". [9]

MIUR and Fonarcom (2016), *Rafforzare il rapporto tra scuola e mondo del lavoro*. [2]

OECD (2017), *Getting Skills Right: France*, OECD Publishing, OECD, https://doi.org/10.1787/25206125 (accessed on 31 March 2018). [5]

Annex A. ANPAL Guidelines

On April 2018, ANPAL published the Guidelines for the management of resources attributed to Trainining Funds ("Linee Guida sulla gestione delle risorse finanziarie attribuite ai fondi paritetici interprofessionali per la formazione continua") (ANPAL, 2018[1]). Some of the most important novelties brought about by the Guidelines are described below. In particular, the Guidelines:

- **Establish criteria for the use of funding**: the Guidelines clarify what channels Training Funds are allowed to use in order to finance training programmes (namely, collective accounts and individual accounts, see Section 2.2). They restrict financing to programmes that clearly identify the competences and skills developed through training, in a view to facilitate skills certification (see Section 5.2). They better regulate (and homogenise) the process for engaging social partners in the approval of training plans. Moreover, – in a view to enhance transparency *vis-à-vis* firms – they require Training Funds to better define and publish the criteria (e.g. deadlines; selection process criteria) through which resources are allocated to training plans *via* public calls (*avvisi*).
- **Impose all Training Funds to establish a standardised internal regulatory framework**: the Guidelines require all Training Funds to develop and publish online an internal regulatory framework – based on a standard format developed and shared by ANPAL – that clarifies the roles of different actors involved in the management and allocation of financial resources, as well as the procedures for the monitoring (both *in itinere* and *ex-post*) of TF-sponsored training activities.
- **Improve transparency and accountability**: the Guidelines require Training Funds to publish online, on a regular basis, information related to how funding is being used – *e.g.* how budget is allocated between training programmes and administrative costs.
- **Delineate the responsibilities of ANPAL:** the Guidelines identify what is the role of ANPAL over the monitoring of the organisation, management, and report-back activities of Training Funds.
- **Make the rules around "portability" stricter and clearer**: the Guidelines re-affirm the principle of portability – according to which firms have the right to switch to one Training Fund to another at any given time – and clarify that internal regulatory framework cannot be used to modify or limit the implementation of such a right (see Section 5.3).
- **Set the scene for the establishment of an integrated information system for adult learning**: the information system will aim to collect data on individuals' training programmes that have been (totally or partially) financed through public resources. Within this context, Training Funds are invited to send – twice a year – information relative to the financial resources, the activities financed, as well as the beneficiaries of training (firms and workers) (including unique identifiers, e.g. fiscal codes) (see Section 5.4).

Annex B. Crosswalk between the Nexus and the OECD Skills for Jobs databases

Section 4.1 aims to assess the extent to which TF-supported training develops the skills that are most in demand in the Italian labour market. To do that, the analysis compares the number of TF-supported training programmes that have been completed in each given skill (or thematic area) with the degree by which that skill is in shortage/surplus in the Italian labour market. The information used for these two indicators draws from two different data sources: information on the number of TF-supported training programmes draws from the Nexus database (see Section 5.4); while information on the skills shortage/surplus indicators draws from the OECD Skills for Jobs database (hereafter S4J database) (see Box 4.1). Because these two data sources apply two different skills taxonomies, the analysis presented in Section 4.1 builds upon a simple crosswalk exercise between the skills taxonomy used by the Nexus database and the one used by the OECD S4J database. The methodology used for the crosswalk, the reference year, and the limitations of the exercise, are described below. The results of the crosswalk are presented in Table A B.1.

Methodology: The Nexus database contains information on various characteristics of TF-supported training programmes, including information on the types of skills that the training programmes aim to develop, using the taxonomy "Fields of Education and Training" - Eurostat, 1999 (MLPS, ISFOL, MFI, ITALIALAVORO, n.a.[2]). The OECD S4J database contains information on the skills that are in shortage/surplus in the labour market, using the occupation-skills taxonomy developed by O*NET (OECD, 2017[3]). Comparing the *definitions* of the skills taxonomies adopted in the Nexus database, with those adopted in the OECD S4J database, it is possible to generate a crosswalk between the two databases. Table A B.1 presents the result of the crosswalk. For almost all skills items contained in the Nexus database, it is possible to build a 1-1 match with a skills item contained in the OECD S4J database. For some skills items, however, it is not possible to develop a 1-1 correspondence. For example, the description of the skills item *Personal Skills* ("Sviluppo delle abilità personali") contained in the Nexus database corresponds to the description of four different skills items included in the OECD S4J database, namely: (i) *Complex Problem Solving*; (ii) *Basic Skills (content)*; (iii) *Basic Skills (Process)*; (iv) *Social Skills*. For the calculation of the skills shortage/surplus indicator, the average of these four skills items is calculated, for every given year. Likewise, the description of the skills item *Manufacturing and Production* contained in the OECD S4J database corresponds to the description of two different skills items included in the Nexus database, namely: (i) *Manufacturing and Production (agriculture and fishery)* ("Tecniche e tecnologie di produzione dell'agricoltura, della zootecnica e della pesca"); and (ii) *Manufacturing and Production (construction)* ("Tecniche e tecnologie di produzione della manifattura e delle costruzioni"). For the calculation of the indicator on the number of TF-supported training programmes (by skill), the sum of these two skills items is used. In some cases it is not possible to map the skills items contained in the Nexus database into the OECD S4J database, because no corresponding skills item could be identified in the latter. This is the case for four skills items, namely: (i) *Knowledge of the workplace* ("Conoscenza del contesto lavorativo"); (ii) *Foreign language, Italian for foreigners* ("Lingue straniere, italiano per stranieri"); (iii) *Occupational health and safety* ("Salute e sicurezza sul lavoro"); (iv) *Environmental protection* ("Salvaguardia ambientale"). These skills items, included in the Nexus database, do not find any correspondence in the OECD S4J database, and are therefore excluded from the analysis presented in Section 4.1.

Reference year: All data presented in Section 4.1 refer to 2015, with the exception of regional data, for which 2016 data are used. This choice is simply driven by data availability. Indeed, while the latest data available contained in the Nexus database (both at the national and regional level) refer to 2016, latest data available contained in the OECD S4J database refer to 2015 for indicators at the national level, and 2016 for indicators at the regional level.

Limitations of the crosswalk exercise: There are two key limitations of the crosswalk exercise. First of all, the OECD S4J database includes a high level of disaggregation of skills, which encompasses a total of 135 skills items; the Nexus database, on the other hand, contains only 14 skills items. This means that the vast majority of the skills items contained in the OECD S4J database cannot be mapped into the Nexus database. Because only a limited number of skills items are available in the Nexus database, this may also lead survey respondents (Training Funds) to record information in an imprecise way, e.g. attributing the skills item that more closely describe the skills developed by the TF-supported training programme, whenever a more adequate skills item option is not available. Secondly, the crosswalk exercise between the Nexus and the OECD S4J database is based on a simple comparison of the descriptions of the skills item, which are by definition not identical. Like any other crosswalk exercise, the crosswalk exercise presented in this report is therefore imperfect and results should be taken with caution.

Table A B.1. Crosswalk between the Nexus and the OECD Skills for Jobs databases

Codes "Fields of Education and Training" in the Nexus database	Skills items in the Nexus database (Italian)	Skills items in the OECD S4J database (English)	Skills items used in this report (English)
347	Conoscenza del contesto lavorativo	n.a.	n.a.
343, 344	Contabilità, finanza	Economics and Accounting	Knowledge of Economics and Accounting
n.a.	Dato non dichiarato	n.a.	n.a.
345	Gestione aziendale (risorse umane, qualità, ecc) e amministrazione	Administration and Management	Knowledge of Administration and Management
481, 482	Informatica	Computers and Electronics	Knowledge of Computers and Electronics
346	Lavoro d'ufficio e di segreteria	Clerical	Clerical Knowledge
222, 223	Lingue straniere, italiano per stranieri	n.a.	n.a.
862	Salute e sicurezza sul lavoro	n.a.	n.a.
850, 851, 852	Salvaguardia ambientale	n.a.	n.a.
090	Sviluppo delle abilità personali	Complex Problem Solving Basic Skills (Content) Basic Skills (Process) Social Skills	Personal skills
From 620 to 640	Tecniche e tecnologie di produzione dell'agricoltura, della zootecnica e della pesca	Manufacturing and Production	Knowledge of Manufacturing and Production
From 520 to 582	Tecniche e tecnologie di produzione della manifattura e delle costruzioni	Manufacturing and Production	Knowledge of Manufacturing and Production
811, 812, 813 815, 840, 853, 861	Tecniche, tecnologie e metodologie per l'erogazione di servizi economici	Customer and Personal Service	Knowledge of Customer and Personal Service
From 720 to 762	Tecniche, tecnologie e metodologie per l'erogazione di servizi sanitari e sociali	Health Services	Knowledge of Health Services
341, 342	Vendita, marketing	Sales and Marketing	Knowledge of Sales and Marketing

ORGANISATION FOR ECONOMIC CO-OPERATION AND DEVELOPMENT

The OECD is a unique forum where governments work together to address the economic, social and environmental challenges of globalisation. The OECD is also at the forefront of efforts to understand and to help governments respond to new developments and concerns, such as corporate governance, the information economy and the challenges of an ageing population. The Organisation provides a setting where governments can compare policy experiences, seek answers to common problems, identify good practice and work to co-ordinate domestic and international policies.

The OECD member countries are: Australia, Austria, Belgium, Canada, Chile, the Czech Republic, Denmark, Estonia, Finland, France, Germany, Greece, Hungary, Iceland, Ireland, Israel, Italy, Japan, Korea, Latvia, Lithuania, Luxembourg, Mexico, the Netherlands, New Zealand, Norway, Poland, Portugal, the Slovak Republic, Slovenia, Spain, Sweden, Switzerland, Turkey, the United Kingdom and the United States. The European Union takes part in the work of the OECD.

OECD Publishing disseminates widely the results of the Organisation's statistics gathering and research on economic, social and environmental issues, as well as the conventions, guidelines and standards agreed by its members.

OECD PUBLISHING, 2, rue André-Pascal, 75775 PARIS CEDEX 16
(81 2019 05 1 P) ISBN 978-92-64-31196-1 – 2019

www.ingramcontent.com/pod-product-compliance
Ingram Content Group UK Ltd.
Pitfield, Milton Keynes, MK11 3LW, UK
UKHW051506290926
15471UKWH00008B/1461

9 789264 311961